THE AMERICAN NEGRO

THE AMERICAN NEGRO

A CHRONOLOGY AND FACT BOOK

by IRVING J. SLOAN

OCEANA PUBLICATIONS, INC.

DOBBS FERRY, NEW YORK

1965

50339

Dedication

There appeared in the *New Yorker* recently a cartoon showing a man researching at a library while a young child pulled at his jacket pleading, "Please, daddy, come home to us." This might very well have been my own youngster, Philip, reflecting both his and my wife Esther's feelings while I indulged myself at the Schomberg Library in Harlem while preparing this manuscript! To these two, then, some expression of thanks for their patience in enduring my long hours at task.

I must also express gratitude to the remarkable co-operation of the staff of Schomberg, a branch of the New York Public Library system, which is devoted exclusively to Negro life and literature. Finally, to the public school system of Scarsdale, New York, whose grant enabled me to spend a full summer studying the history of the Negro in America so that I might bring and share this knowledge with the teachers and students of Scarsdale.

Contents

Introduction

No one can measure the influence or the impact of history on the minds of men. It is certain, however, that the kind of historical treatment—or the lack of it—which the Negro in America has received under the guise of "historical scholarship" has made no small contribution in establishing and perpetuating one of our society's most serious problems: racial discrimination. For the fact is that by omission and commission the history of the American Negro has served to reinforce notions among whites of their superiority and among Negroes of their inferiority.

Dr. John Hope Franklin has distinguished "between what has actually happened and what those who have written history have *said* has happened." He goes on to hail the changes that have occurred in the writing of the history of the Negro in recent years. Indeed, these changes are even more dramatic than the very events themselves that the writers have been describing. "For the first time in the history of the United States, there is a striking resemblance between what historians are writing and what has actually happened in the history of the American Negro.

This small volume presents chronologically and factually the broad sweep of American Negro history. There is no attempt here to amplify or to interpret. For the most part, a book of this nature serves as a quick, handy and, hopefully, reliable reference work. Having located a person or event of interest, the reader can seek out the full story in any number of books which are filling the shelves of literature on Negro life and history.

Compact as the present work is, one can yet come to have an appreciation of the background and the contribution of the Negro in American life by surveying its contents.

The reader will learn at once that Negro history in America does not begin with the first cargo of slaves which was landed in Jamestown in 1619. It begins at the very beginning of American history with the coming of the European explorers. Scholars, indeed, contend that Columbus' pilot was a Negro. But in any case there is no historical doubt that the discoverer of the Pacific Ocean, Balboa, brought with him 30 Negroes whose assistance was invaluable. Cortez was accompanied by a Negro, who, finding in his rations of rice some grains of wheat, planted them as an experiment and thereby introduced wheat raising in the Western Hemisphere. Negroes participated in the exploration of Guatemala and the conquest of Chile, Peru, and Venezuela. Negroes were with Ayllon in 1526 in his expedition from the Florida Peninsula northward and took a part in the establishment of the settlement of San Miguel, near what is now Jamestown, Virginia. Negroes accompanied Narvarez on his ill-fated adventure in 1526 and continued with Cabeza de Vaca, his successor, through what is now the southwestern part of the United States. There Estevancio, a Negro, discovered Cibola, "the seven cities" of the Zuni Indians. Matthew A. Henson, the last to appear in the role of explorer, was chosen by Commodore Peary to accompany him to the North Pole.

The first important contribution of the Negro to the development of America was labor. First as indentured servants and then after being debased to the status of slaves, Negroes supplied the demand for labor demanded by the expansion of trade in the commercial revolution of the modern era. Negroes cleared the forests of the Southland, drained the swamps, prepared the soil for the production of its staples, and dug from the earth nuggets of precious metals. In all sections of America appeared Negro mechanics and artisans, using the skill which was natural to the African even in his native land. These Negro workers shod horses, cast farming implements, made vehicles, constructed boats, and built railroads.

At the same time the Negro showed inventive genius in producing labor-saving devices. Negroes assisted Eli Whitney in his experiments with the cotton gin and McCormick with his reaper. James Forten perfected a machine for handling sails; Henry Blair patented two corn harvesters; Granville T. Woods stimulated industry with his electrical patents; Elijah McCoy brought machinery nearer to perfection with his lubricating devices; Norbert Rillieux revolutionized the manufacture of sugar with his vacuum pan; and Jan E. Matzeliger revolutionized the shoe industry with the lasting device for making shoes with machinery.

While helping to develop the country, the Negro has done his share in defending it. As this Chronology relates again and again, the Negro has acquitted himself with honor in all American wars. They served with the Colonial forces and helped shape the destiny of America. They followed the British standard during the Seven Years War until Montcalm was vanquished by Wolfe on the Plains of Abraham, thereby making English institutions possible in America.

In the American Revolution some 3,000 Negroes fought on the American side with distinction. Negroes were honored as heroes at Bunker Hill and Stony Point. George Washington praised the Negro soldier. Even more fulsome praise was given the Negro soldier by Andrew Jackson after the Battle of New Orleans in 1815; for during the War of 1812 Negroes also fought with impressive distinction.

The great social and political issue of the years following was the question of slavery in 19th century America. Negro newspapers, such as *Freedom's Journal* and *Walker's Appeal,* and Negro leaders, such as Douglass, Garnet, Ward and Pennington, were in the forefront of the abolition movement which brought the nation in the direction of freedom and equality for all.

The Civil War began as a war to save the Union and succeeded also, in destroying slavery. Again the Negro participated in promoting democracy in America. Over two hundred thousand Negroes fought with the Union forces. History confirms the deeds of heroism performed by individual Negro soldiers as well as the significant contribution they made to final victory in terms of numbers alone.

The achievements of the Negro in the theatre, literature, music and the arts through the present day are too familiar to warrant recapitulation here. His role in the wars this country has fought and still fights in this century are also well-known if not always well-recognized. Our Chronology here records all this.

What is perhaps most significant and exciting is to note how in the last decade the events and the people involved in present-day Negro history in the making are largely related to the Negroes struggle on their own behalf for full equality in American society. Coupled with this series of events is the ever-increasing "firsts" among Negroes—the "first" Negro to appear with the Metropolitan Opera; the "first" Negro to enter the Major Leagues in baseball; the "first" Negro to enter a Southern state university, and on and on and on.

And as we see Negroes enter politics and public office our knowledge of Negro history will serve as reassuring evidence that they bring to American public life a background of positive achievements when given the opportunity. During the Reconstruction, contrary to biased and now generally repudiated "history," the Negro gave a good account of himself as a citizen and as a statesman. The majority of the Negro leaders of that day advocated high ideals. The participation of the Negro in the affairs of the Government was denounced and opposed from the very beginning; but despite the mire of corruption into which the Negroes were drawn by the white men who profited at the expense of the freedmen, the Negro demonstrated his capacity for citizenship and his right to all of the honors within the gift of the United States. Indeed, the Negro had never imposed upon government such colossal evidences of corruption and scandal as the "credit mobilier," the "whiskey ring," the "Tweed ring" and many others which were recorded throughout the country during the same period.

It is the very aim of a book like this to make some small contribution toward setting down the historical achievements and therefore historical truths concerning such a large part of our American people, the Negro. In proposing this, one need not suggest that we learn less about the great leaders and episodes already recognized and honored in American history. It only means that we include in our knowledge the role of the Negro in our history. Having that knowledge will give us the understanding that the Negroes' long "advance from slavery to freedom and from freedom to equality has significantly involved and affected the lives of millions of Americans of all races and all generations." Such an understanding will make it possible to accept Negro fellow citizens as equals—and this, after all, is what the most critical issue of our democratic society is all about today.

Chronology

1442 First African slave brought to Lisbon, Portugal.

1492 Pedro Alonzo Nino, said by many scholars to have been a Negro, arrived with Columbus as one of his pilots. Oct. 12.

1513 Balboa's expedition to the Pacific included thirty Negroes who were instrumental in clearing the way between the two oceans. April.

1517 Bishop Las Casas influenced the Spanish government to allow Spaniards to import twelve Negroes each to encourage immigration to the New World.

1526 The first slave revolt took place in the first United States settlement which contained slaves—an area in present-day South Carolina. April 22.

1538 Estevanico (Little Stephen), a Negro explorer, led expedition from Mexico and discovered Arizona and New Mexico.

1539 Negroes accompanied De Soto on his journey to the Mississippi.

1540 The second settler in the state of Alabama was a Negro who was with De Soto's expedition. Liking the land, he settled among the Indians.

1562 John Hawkins carried slaves from Portuguese Africa to Spanish America.

1

1565   Negroes were with Mendez in founding St. Augustine, Florida.

1619   A Dutch ship anchored at Jamestown, Virginia, with a cargo of "twenty Negras"—thus began Negro history in English America. Aug.

1620   The first public school for Negroes and Indians in Virginia was established.

1624   William Tucker was the first Negro child born and baptized in English America at Jamestown, Virginia.

1638   First Negro slaves were brought into New England.

1641   Massachusetts was the first colony to recognize slavery as a legal institution.

1644   Marriage of Antony van Angola and Lucie d'Angola was the first in Negro life to be recorded in America on Manhattan Island.

1645   Voyage of the *Rainbowe,* the first American slave ship.

1661   First individual petition of a Negro for his freedom addressed to the colony of New Netherland was granted.

1662   Virginia enacted a statute making slavery hereditary, following the status of the mother.

1663   The first major slave rebellion in colonial America took place in Gloucester, Virginia.

1664   Maryland passed a law preventing marriages between English women and Negroes; several of the colonies followed suit soon thereafter.

1671   Maryland passed Act declaring that conversion of slaves to Christianity did not affect their slave status.

1672   The King of England chartered the Royal African Company which came to dominate the world slave trade.

1688   Quakers of Germantown, Pennsylvania, made the first formal protest against slavery in the Western hemisphere. Feb. 18.

1704 Elias Nau, a Frenchman, opened the first school for Negroes in New York City.

1705 Virginia enacted a law permitting owners to list people as property.

1712 Early slave revolt in New York City. April 7.
Pennsylvania passed first legislation to prevent importation of slaves.

1713 Anthony Benezet, a teacher of Negroes and leading abolitionist in Pennsylvania, born.

1715 Francisco Xavier de Luna Victoria was the first Negro to become bishop in America (Panama).

1720 Jupiter Hammon of Long Island, the first Negro American writer, was born in Africa.

1731 Benjamin Banneker, colonial mathematician and astronomer, was born near Baltimore, Maryland. Nov. 9.

1733 Samuel Sewall published the first anti-slavery tract which appeared in the colonies, "The Selling of Joseph."

1741 A serious slave revolt in New York City resulted in the hanging of eighteen Negroes. March-April.

1745 A Negro, Jean Baptiste Pointe Du Saible, who established a trading post which later became the city of Chicago, was born in Haiti.

1746 Toussaint L'ouverture, revolutionary leader of Haiti, born. May 20.

1747 Absalom Jones, first Negro minister ordained in America, born a slave in Sussex, Delaware.

1748 Prince Hall, successful businessman and founder of Negro Free Masonry, born.

1750 Crispus Attucks, first martyr of the American Revolution, escaped from his master in Framingham, Massachusetts. Sept. 30.

1753 Scipio Moorhead, earliest known Negro artist, born.
Lemuel Haynes, first Negro to serve as pastor in white congregation in the United States, born. July 18.

3

1756   John Woolman began his campaign against slavery. May 12.

1758   Frances Williams, first Negro college graduate in Western hemisphere, published Latin poems. April 17.

1759   Paul Cuffee, business leader and philanthropist, born. Jan. 17.

1760   Richard Allen, founder and bishop of the African Methodist Church, born a slave near Philadelphia. Feb. 14.

1761   Phillis Wheatley, poetess of the American Revolutionary period, arrived in Boston harbor on a slave ship.

1761   Jupiter Hammon published "An Evening Thought." Dec. 15.

1762   James Derham, the first recognized Negro medical doctor in America, born in Philadelphia.

1768   Rev. James Varick, first Superintendent and bishop of the African Methodist Episcopal Zion Church, born in New York City.

1770   Crispus Attucks was the first of the five men to be killed in the Boston Massacre. March 5.

Anthony Benezet opened school for Negroes in Philadelphia. June 28.

1772   Lord Mansfield handed down his decision in the *Somerset* case against the existence of slavery on English soil. This case stimulated requests for legislative action against slavery in New England. June 22.

1773   George Leile and Andrew Bryan organized the first Negro Baptist Church in Savannah, Georgia.

Bill Richmond, father of modern prizefighting, born in Statin Island.

Jean Baptiste Point du Saible, first permanent settler in Chicago, purchased the house and land of Jean Baptiste Millet at "Old Peoria Fort."

Massachusetts slaves petitioned the state legislature for their freedom. Jan. 6.

1774 Continental Congress voted an agreement not to import any slaves after December 1.

1775 Benjamin Franklin was elected president upon the establishment of the first abolition society organized in America by the Quakers in Philadelphia. April 14.

Negro soldiers fought in the Battle of Bunker Hill. Peter Salem, who shot down Major Pitcairn, was one of the heroes of the day. June 17.

Continental Congress passed a resolution barring Negroes from the American Revolutionary Army. Oct. 13.

Lord Dunmore, royal governor of Virginia, issued a proclamation offering freedom to all male slaves who joined the British forces. Nov. 7.

General George Washington, alarmed by the response to Dunmore's Proclamation, ordered recruiting officers to accept free Negroes. December 31.

Thomas Paine wrote his first published essay in the cause of abolition in a Pennsylvania newspaper.

The first lodge of Negro Free Masons was founded by Prince Hall. July 3.

1776 Continental Congress approved Washington's action of permitting free Negroes to enlist in the Revolutionary Army. Jan. 16.

Mason-Dixon line named for two English surveyors. Feb. 18.

Phillis Wheatley was invited by General Washington to visit him at his headquarters in Cambridge, Mass., so that he might express appreciation for her poem in his honor. Feb. 28.

The Declaration of Independence was adopted without section denouncing slave trade, one of the original grievances against the British king. July 4.

Two Negroes, Prince Whipple and Oliver Cromwell, were with General Washington on Christmas day when he crossed the Delaware. Dec. 25.

Gabriel Prosser, leader of historic slave revolt in Virginia, born a slave.

1777   Vermont was the first state to abolish slavery. July 2.

1778   Four hundred Negroes held off fifteen hundred British in the Battle of Rhode Island. Aug. 28.

More than three thousand Negroes fought in the Revolutionary War.

1779   Twenty slaves petitioned the New Hampshire legislature to abolish slavery. Nov. 12.

Anthony Wayne's victory at Stony Point made possible by the spying of "Pompey," a Negro soldier.

1780   Pennsylvania passed a law for the gradual abolition of slavery.

Lott Carey, an early Negro Baptist missionary, born.

First license to a Negro preacher granted.

1783   Revolutionary War soldiers, "The Black Regiment," disbanded at Saratoga, N. Y. June 13.

Treaty of Paris, Article VII, promised return to Americans all Negro slaves.

1784   North Carolina answered petition of Edward Griffin, Negro Revolutionary soldier, commended his meritorious service, and freed him. May 4.

Phillis Wheatley died in Boston. Dec. 5.

1785   Constitutional Convention approved three clauses protecting slavery. Sept. 17.

David Walker, first Negro to attack slavery in published writings, born in Wilmington, North Carolina. Sept. 28.

1786   Arthur Tappan, leading white abolitionist, born. May 22.

6

1787 Congress added a provision to the Northwest Ordinance forbidding slavery in the territory covered by the Ordinance. July 13.

First free school in New York City, the African Free School, opened. Nov. 1.

1788 Andrew Bryan ordained the first pastor of the First African Baptist Church organized in Savannah, Georgia. Jan. 19-20.

1789 Josiah Henson, the model for Harriet Beecher Stowe's "Uncle Tom," of the famed novel, was born a slave in Maryland; he later became a leading abolitionist orator. June 15.

1790 The Pennsylvania Abolition Society petitioned Congress to abolish slavery. Feb. 3.

Samuel Cornish born in Delaware.

First United States census showed Negro population of 757,181, with 59,557 free.

1791 Benjamin Banneker was appointed, at the suggestion of Thomas Jefferson, to serve as member of commission headed by L'enfant to lay out plans for the city of Washington in District of Columbia.

1792 Antoine Blanc founded the first Negro Catholic sisterhood in the United States. Oct. 11.

1793 Benjamin Lundy, colonizationist, born. Jan. 4.

First fugitive slave law enacted by Congress, making it criminal offense to protect a fugitive slave. Feb. 12.

Eli Whitney invented cotton gin which influenced mass importation of Negroes and thereby strengthened slavery as an institution.

Dr. Benjamin Rush of Philadelphia sought the aid of the Negroes of the city to administer medicines and care for the sick during yellow fever epidemc. It was believed that Negroes were immune.

7

1794 Richard Allen organized African Methodist Episcopal Church. June 10.

St. Thomas Church, Philadelphia, first Episcopal Negro Congregation, organized. Oct. 12.

1796 Zion Methodist Church organized in New York City.

1797 First petition by Negroes was submitted to Congress protesting a North Carolina law requiring Negroes who were freed by their Quaker masters to be returned to the state and to their slavery status. The petition was rejected. Jan. 30.

Sojourner Truth, leading abolitionist figure in Negro history, born a slave in Hurley, New York.

1798 Thaddeus Koscuisko, Polish patriot, left will providing for education of Negroes. May 5.

James P. Beckwourth, scout for General Fremont and noted pioneer and explorer of the West, born in Virginia.

Levi Coffin, organizer of the underground railroad, born. Oct. 28.

1799 Alexander Pushkin, Russian Negro poet, born in Moscow.

1800 The free Negroes of Philadelphia presented a petition to Congress opposing the slave trade, the Fugitive Act of 1793, and the institution of slavery itself. Jan. 2.

Gabriel Prosser, a Virginian slave, was betrayed in his plot to lead thousands of slaves in an attack on Richmond, Virginia. Dozens of slaves were imprisoned or hanged on the spot, and Gabriel himself was publicly hanged. Aug. 30.

John Brown born in Torrington, Connecticut. May 9.

James Derham began practicing medicine in New Orleans.

Nat Turner, destined to lead another major slave rebellion, born a slave in Southampton County, Virginia. Oct. 2.

1802 Alexander Dumas, French novelist of Negro extraction, born in France.

1803 Lunsford Lane, noted lecturer for the American Anti-

Slavery Society, born a slave in Raleigh, North Carolina.

Toussaint L'ouverture, slave leader of Haitian Revolution, died. April 27.

1804   The Ohio legislature enacted the first of the "Black Laws" which restricted rights and movements of Negroes in the North; other Northern states soon passed similar legislation. Jan. 5.

1805   Benjamin Banneker died. Oct. 9.

William E. Dodge, proponent of Negro education, born.

1806   Maria Weston Chapman, abolitionist, born. July 25.

Norbert Rillieux, inventor and scientist, born in New Orleans.

1807   British Parliament abolished the slave trade. March 25.

Ira F. Aldridge, one of the greatest Shakespearean actors of his time, was born in New York City.

Charles Bennet Ray, minister, editor, lecturer, organizer, and abolitionist, born in Massachusetts.

1808   Federal law barring the African slave trade went into effect. Jan. 1.

1809   Abraham Lincoln born in Harden County, Kentucky. Feb. 12.

James W. C. Pennington, leader in the Free Negro Convention Movement which outlined an ideology and tactics for the Negro protest in the 19th century, born a slave in Washington County, Maryland.

Abyssinian Baptist Church organized in New York City. July 5.

1810   Charles Lenox Remond, leader of the American Anti-Slavery Society, born in Massachusetts. Feb. 1.

Thomy Lafon, philanthropist who supported the American Anti-Slavery society and the underground railroad, born in New Orleans.

Theodore Parker, liberal minister, born. Aug. 24.

Cassius M. Clay, Kentucky emancipationist, born. Oct. 19.
David Ruggles, founder of *Mirror of Liberty*—first Negro periodical—born.

1811—Charles Sumner, great New England advocate of Negro rights, born. Jan. 6.

Rev. Daniel A. Payne, African Methodist Episcopalian, who established Union Seminary near Columbus, Ohio, born. Feb. 24.

Harriet Beecher Stowe, author of *Uncle Tom's Cabin,* born. June 14.

1812   Martin R. Delaney, newspaper editor and author, Union Army Major, born. May 6.

George Washington, pioneer, humanitarian and founder of Centralia, Washington, born a slave. Aug. 15.

The Union Church of Africans, organized and incorporated. Sept. 25.

Bishop Richard Allen and Reverend Absalom Jones were requested to help organize defenses for Philadelphia against the British who had recently attacked Washington.

John Johnson, one of many Negroes who served in the Navy on the Great Lakes during the War of 1812, was described by his commander after his death in a naval battle: "When America has such tars, she has little to fear from tyrants of the ocean."

1813   Henry Ward Beecher, promoter for equal rights, born. June 24.

James McCune Smith born of slaves in New York City.

1814   Daniel Reaves Goodloe, North Carolinan emancipationist, born. May 28.

General Andrew Jackson appealed to free Negroes to fight as part of the militia. Sept. 21.

New York legislature authorized the raising of two Negro regiments. As a result 2000 Negroes were enlisted and sent to the army at Sacketts Harbor. Oct. 24.

1815   Henry Highland Garnet, minister, abolitionist, and diplomat, born a slave in Kent County, Maryland. Dec. 23.

Myrtilla Miner, founder of Miner's Teachers College, born. March 4.

1816   The African Methodist Episcopal Church became independent of jurisdictional control by higher all-white bodies. April 9.

Peter Salem, hero of Bunker Hill, died. Aug. 16.

John Jones, "the most prominent citizen of Chicago" during his lifetime, born in Greene County, North Carolina.

The Seminole Wars led by General Andrew Jackson began with an attack on a fort in western Florida which contained hundreds of runaway slaves living among the Creek and Seminole Indians who occupied it.

Bishop Daniel Wayne, reformer and educator, born.

1817   Free Negroes in the large cities held protest meetings against the American Colonization Society's efforts to "exile us from the land of our nativity." Jan.

Frederick Douglass, orator, editor and statesman, was born a slave in Talbot County, Maryland. Feb. 14.

Victor Sejour, Negro Creole poet and dramatist, born. June 2.

The American Colonization Society was organized under the leadership of John C. Calhoun and Henry Clay. Its purpose was to transport free Negroes to Africa. Dec. 28.

Samuel Ringald Ward, the "Black Daniel Webster," was born in Maryland; he was one of the most noted Negro abolitionists. Oct. 17.

James Forten, Negro abolitionist, was chairman of the First Negro Convention held in Philadelphia.

Paul Cuffee, Negro shipbuilder and African colonizer, died.

1818   Philadelphia free Negroes established the Pennsylvania Augustine Society, "for the education of people of colour."

St. Philip's Episcopal Church was opened for Negroes in New York City.

Absolom Jones died. Feb. 13.

Charles L. Reason, Negro writer, born. July 21.

1820   Missouri Compromise enacted; prohibited slavery north of Missouri. March 3.

Harriet Tubman born a slave in Dorchester County, Maryland.

The American Colonization Society founded Liberia, a Negro Republic in West Africa.

1821   Lott Carey, minister and pioneer leader in Liberia, sailed for that country. Jan. 23.

African Methodist Episcopal Zion Church founded in New York City. June 21.

William Still, author of *Underground Railroad* and leading underground spokesman, born in New Jersey. Oct. 7.

Alexander Crummell, one of the most highly educated Negroes of his time, born.

1822   Denmark Vesey planned one of the most extensive slave revolts ever recorded. The plot was betrayed and Vesey together with thirty-six others, were executed. July 2.

Hiram R. Revels, first Negro United States Senator, was born free in Fayetteville, North Carolina. Sept. 27.

Rev. John Gloucester, first Negro minister of a Presbyterian church, died.

1823   Thomas Wentworth Higginson, commander of Negro soldiers, born.

1825   Frances Ellen Watkins Harper, poet and orator, born in Baltimore, Maryland.

1826   James Madison Bell, poet and abolitionist, born free at Gallipolis, Ohio. April 3.

John Russworm was the first Negro to graduate from an American college when he received his degree from Bowdoin College, Maine.

Ira F. Aldridge made his London debut in *Othello;* he never returned to America and became the most famous Shakespearean actor of his time on the continent.

1827 Slavery was officially abolished in New York State. July 4. *Freedom's Journal,* the first Negro newspaper, was published in New York City by John Russworm and Samuel Cornish. March 16.

1828 Lott Carey, first missionary to Liberia, died. April 1.

1829 *Walker's Appeal,* militant anti-slavery pamphlet published by David Walker, was distributed throughout the country and aroused the Negroes and provoked slave-holders. Jan. 18.
John Mercer Langston born. Dec. 14.

1830 James Augustine Healy, the first Negro Roman Catholic bishop in America, born to an Irish planter and a Negro slave on a plantation near Macon, Georgia. April 6.
S. R. Lowry, religious educator, born. Dec. 9.
United States Bureau of the Census reported 3,777 Negro heads of families who owned slaves; most of these Negroes lived in Louisiana, Maryland, Virginia, North Carolina, South Carolina, and Virginia.
Dan Rice, famous white "blackface" minstrel began performing "Jump Jim Crow" song-dance—from which song the words "Jim Crow" came to be applied to legal segregation.

1831 The first issue of the *Liberator* was published by William Lloyd Garrison. Jan. 1.
Nat Turner led the greatest slave rebellion in the United States in Virginia; the whole South was thrown into panic and more than one hundred and sixty whites and Negroes were killed before the revolt ended. Aug.
Bishop John Walden, advocate of Negro education, born. Feb. 11.
Nat Turner executed. Nov. 11.

1832 Joseph P. Rainey, Negro Congressman from South Carolina, born. June 21.

Dr. Edward W. Blyden, distinguished scholar and diplomat, president of Liberia College, born. Aug. 3.

The New England Anti-Slavery Society was established by twelve whites at the African Baptist Church in Boston.

1833 Oberlin College opened and admitted Negroes at the outset.

Frederick Douglass escaped from his master and fled to New York.

The Philadelphia Negro Library was organized.

Henry Macneil Turner, a bishop of the African Methodist Church and colonizationist, was free-born in Abbeville, South Carolina.

The American Anti-Slavery Society was organized in Philadelphia by Negro and white abolitionists. Dec. 4.

1834 Slavery abolshed in the British Empire. Aug. 1.

Henry Blair was the first Negro to receive a patent for an invention, a corn harvester. Oct. 14.

South Carolina enacted a law prohibiting the teaching of free or slave Negro children.

Negro youth leaders formed the Garrison Literary and Benevolent Association of New York in order "to begin, in early life, to assist each other to alleviate the afflicted. . ."

The first school for Negroes in Cincinnati, paid for by themselves, was opened.

Bishop Isaac Lane, founder of Lane College in Jackson, Tennessee, born.

Anti-abolition riot broke out in Philadelphia and continued for three days and nights.

1835 Fifth National Negro Convention resolved to recommend that Negroes remove the word "African" from the names of their institutions and organizations, and also to abandon the use of the word "colored" when referring to themselves. June 1-5.

John Greenleaf Whittier published his poem, "My Countrymen in Chains."

New York City Negroes formed a vigilance committee to prevent kidnapping of Negroes and to assist fugitive slaves.

William Whipper helped to found the American Moral Reform Society, a Negro abolitionist group.

1836   Theodore S. Wright, first Negro to receive a degree from a theological seminary in the United States (Princeton). Nov. 5.

1837   P.S.B. Pinchback, Negro Reconstructionist statesman in Louisiana, born. May 10.

Robert Gould Shaw, Colonel of the 54th Massachusetts Union Regiment, first Negro company sent from the free states, born in Boston of a "proper" Bostonian family which was deeply committed to the cause of Negro freedom. Oct. 10.

Elijah P. Lovejoy was murdered by a mob in Alton, Illinois, when he refused to stop publishing anti-slavery material. Nov. 7.

James M. Smith, University of Glasgow graduate, conducted pioneer work in the scientific study of race.

William Whipper published "An Address on Non-Resistance to Offensive Aggression"—an article written twelve years before Thoreau's famous essay on non-violence, and more than 125 years before the career of Martin Luther King, Jr.

1838   The first Negro periodical, *Mirror of Freedom*, began publishing in New York City. Aug. 30.

Frederick Douglass escaped from slavery in Baltimore. Sept. 3.

Charles Lenox Remond became first Negro lecturer employed by an anti-slavery society.

1839   Robert Smalls, Civil War hero and Reconstructionist Congressman, born in Beaufort, South Carolina. April 5.

Lunsford Lane of North Carolina made the only abolition speech before a southern audience. April 30.

Benjamin Lundy died. Aug. 22.

Liberty Party, first anti-slavery political party, organized. Nov. 13.

Whites burned the Negro section of Pittsburgh.

The most famous slave revolt aboard a slave ship took place on the Spanish slaver, the *Amistead*. John Quincy Adams, at the age of 73 and out of law practice more than thirty years, argued the case before the United States Supreme Court. Cinque, the young African leader, and his fellow crewmen were freed by the Court.

1840   James M. Turner, a Lincoln University founder, born in Jefferson City, Missouri. May 16.

1841   Blanche Kelso Bruce, only Negro to serve full term in United States Senate, born a slave at Prince Edward County, Virginia. March 1.

President Tyler sent a message to Congress dealing with the suppression of the slave trade. June 1.

Frederick Douglass became lecturer for the Massachusetts Anti-Slavery Society. Aug.

James M. Townsend, first Negro to serve as member of Indiana Legislature, born. Aug. 18.

Slave trader "Creole" was scene of slave revolt. Slaves took over ship and sailed to Bahamas where they were given asylum and freedom. Nov.

1842   Robert Brown Elliott, Reconstruction Congressman from South Carolina, born. Aug. 11.

Charlie Smith, last known slave brought to America, born in Liberia.

James Forten died in Philadelphia.

Capture of George Latimore in Boston precipitated the first of several famous fugitive slave cases which embittered North and South. Boston abolitionists raised enough money to purchase Latimore from his master. Nov. 17.

1843   Sojourner Truth, first Negro woman to become lecturer against slavery, left New York and began her work as an abolitionist. June 1.

Henry Highland Garnet made controversial speech at the National Convention of Colored Men in Buffalo calling for a slave revolt and a general strike. Aug. 22.

Negroes participated in a national political gathering for the first time at a meeting of the Liberty Party convention in Buffalo, New York. Aug. 30.

1844   James Beckwourth discovered a pass through the coast range to the Pacific Ocean which was named for him, *Beckwourth Pass*. April 26.

Elijah J. McCoy, inventor (lubricating cup), born. May 2.

Charles Nash, Congressman from Louisiana, born. May 23.

1845   Macon B. Allen was the first Negro formally admitted to the bar when he passed the examination at Worcester, Massachusetts. May 3.

Narrative of Frederick Douglass published.

Publication of *Les Cenelles,* in French and English, an anthology of poetry by Negro poets of New Orleans.

Frederick Douglass delivered the commencement address at Western Reserve College which was one of the first Negro attempts to refute racism scientifically.

1847   Frederick Douglass began to publish his own newspaper, the *North Star*. Dec. 3.

William Alexander Leidesdorff, Negro businessman, launched the first steamboat to sail in San Francisco Bay; he later built the first hotel in that city.

Dred Scott case initiated in St. Louis Circuit Court. June 30.

1848   Negro blacksmith Lewis Temple invented a Toggle harpoon which became the standard harpoon of the American whaling industry.

William and Ellen Craft escaped from slavery in Georgia in one of the most dramatic escapes of the period. Dec. 26.

1849 Harriet Tubman escaped from slavery in Maryland. July. Archibald H. Grimke, Harvard Law School graduate and author of biographies of Charles Sumner and William Lloyd Garrison, born near Charleston, South Carolina. Aug. 17.

Benjamin Roberts filed the first school integration suit on behalf of his daughter who had been denied admission to the white schools in Boston. The Supreme Court of Massachusetts rejected the suit and established the "separate but equal" doctrine.

"Blind Tom," the greatest musical prodigy of his time, born a slave in Georgia.

1850 Fugitive Slave Law passed by Congress as part of the Compromise of 1850; it offered federal officers a fee for captured slaves. Sept. 18.

1851 William C. Nell published *Services of Colored Americans in the Wars of 1776 and 1812,* the first full-length study of the American Negro.

Walter H. Brooks, distinguished clergyman, born. Aug. 30.

1852 First edition of *Uncle Tom's Cabin* published. March 20. Napoleon issued a decree against the slave trade. March 29.

1853 First Negro YMCA established in Washington, D. C. Jan. 3.

Williams Wells Brown wrote *Clotel,* the first novel by an American Negro.

Publication of Solomon Northrup's *Narrative of a Slave,* one of the most famous of the many narratives written by fugitive slaves telling their stories.

1854 Lincoln University, the first Negro college, was chartered as Ashmond Institute in Chester, Pennsylvania. Jan. 1.

Augustus Tolon, first Negro Catholic priest to serve in the United States, was born in Battle Creek, Missouri. April 1.

Lucey C. Laney, founder of Haines Institute in Augusta, Georgia, born. April 13.

Kansas-Nebraska Act repealed the Missouri Compromise and opened Northern territory to slavery. May 30.

Anthony Burns was returned to slavery in Virginia in spite of an attempt by Boston citizens to purchase his freedom for $1200. June 3.

The Republican Party was created by Free Soilers and Whigs as well as Democrats who were opposed to the extension of slavery.

1855 Negro troops mustered into Confederate service. March 24.

1856 Booker T. Washington born a slave in Franklin County, Virginia. April 5.

Granville T. Woods, inventor of industrial appliances, born. April 23.

Wilberforce University founded by Methodist Episcopal Church. Aug. 30.

1857 Dred Scott decision by the United States Supreme Court opened federal territory to slavery and denied citizenship to American Negroes. May 6.

Dred Scott and his family were freed by the new owner, Taylor Blow. May 26.

1858 Daniel Hale Williams, called the "Father of Negro Hospitals," born in Hollidayburg, Pennsylvania. Jan. 18.

Twelve whites and thirty-four Negroes attended John Brown's anti-slavery convention in Chatham, Canada. May 8.

Charles W. Chestnutt, Negro pioneer novelist, born. June 20.

Lecompton, Kansas constitution, sanctioning slavery, rejected. Aug. 2.

William Wells Brown published *The Escape*, first play written by an American Negro.

1859 Henry O. Tanner, world famous artist, born in Pittsburgh. June 21.

John Brown met for last time with Frederick Douglass at an old quarry in Chambersburg, Pennsylvania. Aug. 19.

John Brown raided Harper's Ferry. Oct. 16.

The last slave ship, *Clothilde*, landed its cargo of slaves at Mobile, Alabama.

Samuel Cornish, one of the first men to approach the race problem from an economic point of view, died.

John Brown hanged at Charles Town, West Virginia. Dec. 2.

1860 George Washington Carver born in Diamond Grove, Missouri.

Abraham Lincoln elected President. Nov. 6.

South Carolina declared herself an "independent commonwealth." Dec. 18.

1861 Robert Smalls (Union Navy pilot) watching preparations for the attack on Fort Sumter, said "this, boys, is the dawn of freedom for our race." April 10.

Confederates attacked Fort Sumter. April 12.

Lincoln issued proclamation calling for 75,000 volunteers from the states. April 15.

Loyal Negro volunteers were not accepted when the first call for troops was made.

Clara Barton with five Negro girls gave aid to the wounded in the passage through Baltimore. April 21.

General B. F. Butler refused to return three escaped slaves as they were "contraband of war." May 24.

General George B. McClellan, Ohio Department, issued orders to suppress any Negro attempts at insurrection. May 26.

Negro Mass Meeting offered to raise an army of 50,000 men and that the women would serve as nurses, etc. May 31.

Hampton Institute's first day, with Mary S. Peake, as the first Negro teacher. Aug. 17.

The Secretary of the Navy authorized the enlistm
Negro slaves later in the year. Sept. 25.

1862   President Lincoln recommended to Congress gradual,
        compensated emancipation. March 6.

        United States Senate passed bill abolishing slavery in the
        District of Columbia. April 4.

        Robert Smalls, Negro pilot, sailed armed Confederate
        steamer, the *Planter*, out of Charleston, South Carolina,
        and presented her to the Unted States Navy. May 13.

        Liberia recognized as a free nation by the United States.
        June 3.

        Lincoln recommended aid to states abolishing slavery.
        July 14.

        The first regular colored troops were enlisted at Leaven-
        worth, Kansas. July 17.

        Anthony Burns, Baptist clergyman whose capture as a
        fugitive slave caused a riot in Boston, died. July 27.

        Charlotte Forten, Negro poet and teacher, arrived in St.
        Helena, South Carolina, to teach Negroes. Oct. 29.

        First African Methodist Episcopal Church established at
        New Bern, North Carolina. Dec. 27.

1863   President Lincoln signed the Emancipation Proclamation.
        Jan. 1.

        The War Department authorized Massachusetts governor
        to recruit Negro troops. The Fifty-fourth Massachusetts
        Volunteers was the first Negro regiment raised in the
        North. Jan. 26.

        Two Negro infantry regiments, First and Second, South
        Carolina, captured and occupied Jacksonville, Florida,
        causing panic along the Southern seaboard. March 10.

        Confederate Congress passed resolution which branded
        Negro troops and their officers criminals; thus captured
        Negro soldiers could be put to death or slavery. May 1.

        Eight Negro regiments played important role in the seige
        of Port Hudson which, with the fall of Vicksburg, gave

the Union control of the Mississippi River and cut the Confederacy into two sections. July 9.

The New York City Draft Riots were the bloodiest in American history. July 13-17.

The Fifty-fourth Massachusetts Volunteers made a charge on Fort Wagner in Charleston Harbor, South Carolina. At least one member of the all-Negro regiment won the Congressional Medal of Honor for his bravery. July 18.

Kelly Miller, author and educator, born. July 18.

Dr. Mary Church Terrell, first president of the National Association of Colored Women, born. Sept. 23.

1864   Famous Battle of Fort Pillow and the massacre of Negro troops after its surrender. April 12.

In a duel between USS *Kearsage* and CSS *Alabama* off the coast of France, a Negro sailor, Joachim Pease, displayed "marked coolness," and won the Congressional Medal of Honor. June 19.

Fugitive slave laws repealed. June 28.

Maryland constitution amended to abolish slavery. July 7.

Although he himself was not certain of actual date, George Washington Carver celebrated his birthday on this date. July 12.

New Orleans *Tribune* began publishing as the first daily Negro newspaper in French and English. Oct. 14.

Richard B. Harrison, featured actor who created the role of "De Lawd" in *Green Pastures*, born. Aug. 28.

Congress passed a bill equalizing for the first time the pay, arms, equipment and medical services of Negro troops.

Charles Young (Colonel), West Point graduate who held the highest rank in his time, born.

"Blind Boone," John W. Boone, a noted musical prodigy, born in Miami, Missouri.

First public school system for Negroes opened in the District of Columbia.

1865   General Lee said that it was "not only expedient but necessary" that the Confederate Army use Negro slaves as soldiers. Jan. 11.

John S. Rock was the first Negro to practice before the United States Supreme Court. Feb. 1.

Henry Highland Garnet was the first Negro to preach in the Capitol delivering a sermon on the abolition of slavery. Feb. 12.

Congress passed a bill giving freedom to wives and children of Negro soldiers. March 3.

The Freedman's Bureau established by Congress to help the newly emancipated slaves. March 13.

Abraham Lincoln died from wounds received when shot at Ford's Theater by actor John Wilkes Booth. April 15.

Two white regiments and a Negro regiment, the 62nd USCT, fought the last action of the Civil War at White's Ranch, Texas. Sergeant Crocket, a Negro, believed to have been the last man to shed blood in the War. May 13.

President Andrew Johnson announced his Reconstruction plan. May 29.

South Carolina abolished slavery. Aug. 27.

Timothy T. Fortune, journalist and founder of the New York *Age,* born. Oct. 3.

Congress passed the Thirteenth Amendment which, on ratification, abolished slavery in the United States. Dec. 18.

Fisk University opened. April 20.

Patrick Henry Healy was the first Negro to win the Doctor of Philosophy degree when he passed his final examination in Louvain, Belgium. July 26.

Matthew A. Henson, Negro explorer who accompanied Peary to the North Pole, born in Charles County, Maryland. August 8.

Edward G. Walker and Charles L. Mitchell were elected to the Massachusetts House of Representatives thus becoming the first Negroes elected to an American legislative assembly.

Ku Klux Klan organized in Tennessee.

Shaw University founded.

Howard University founded as Howard Seminary in Washington, D.C. Nov. 20.

1867 Talladega and Morehouse College opened. Feb.

Peabody Educational Fund established for the South. Feb. 7.

Maggie Lena Walker, the first woman bank president in the United States, born in Richmond, Virginia.

Robert R. Moton, outstanding educator, born. Aug. 26.

William Still led a successful campaign against segregated streetcars in Philadelphia.

Samuel Ringgold Ward died in the British West Indies.

1868 William Edward Burghardt Du Bois born in Great Barrington, Massachusetts. Feb. 23.

Hampton Institute opened. April.

Fourteenth Amendment became part of the Constitution. July 28.

John Hope, educator, born. June 2.

Oscar J. Dunn, ex-slave, became Lieutenant Governor of Louisiana, the highest elective offiice then held by an American Negro. June 13.

1869 Will Marion Cook, famed composer, born. Jan. 27.

Jefferson P. Long from Georgia was seated as the first Negro in the House of Representatives.

The American Anti-Slavery Society was dissolved.

Ebenzer Don Carlos Bennett was the first Negro to receive an appointment in the diplomatic service when he became Minister to Haiti. April 16.

1870 Fifteenth Amendment adopted, giving the Negro the right to vote. March 30.

Thomas Peterson was the first Negro to vote in the United States the day after the Fifteenth Amendment was ratified.

Robert S. Abbott, founder of the Chicago *Defender*, born on St. Simon's Island off the coast of Georgia. Nov. 24.

James W. C. Pennington died.

Freedman's Bureau expired by law.

1871 James Weldon Johnson, poet, educator, civil rights fighter, first Negro consul to Nicaragua, born in Jacksonville, Florida. June 17.

Fisk Jubilee Singers made their first appearances under the direction of George L. White.

Oscar De Priest, first Negro Congressman elected from a northern state (Illinois), born.

1872 Booker T. Washington entered Hampton Institute.

Paul Laurence Dunbar, nationally-known poet and short story writer, born in Dayton, Ohio. June 27.

John H. Conyers was the first Negro admitted to the United States Naval Academy. Oct. 21.

P.B.S. Pinchback became Acting Governor of Louisiana on the impeachment of the Governor. Dec. 11.

First Negro police officer appointed in Chicago.

Charlotte E. Ray, the first Negro woman lawyer, graduated from Howard University Law School; she was first woman to graduate from a university law school.

William Still published the records of the fugitive slaves in the classic, *Underground Railroad*.

1873 Slavery abolished in Puerto Rico. March 23.

John W. Work, musician, Negro folk singer expert, born. Aug. 6.

W. C. Handy, "Father of the Blues," born in Florence, Alabama. Nov. 16.

Richard T. Greener, first Negro graduate of Harvard University, named professor of metaphysics at the University of South Carolina.

1874 William C. Nell died. May 25.

Patrick Henry Healy, Negro, inaugurated as President of

Georgetown University, oldest Catholic university in the United States. July 31.

1875 Negroes massacred at Hamburg, South Carolina. July 9.

Civil Rights Bill enacted by Congress contained equal accommodations provisions. March 1.

Mary McLeod Bethune, noted educator, born in Mayesville, South Carolina. July 10.

Blanche K. Bruce became a member of the United States Senate from Mississippi, the only Negro to serve a full term in the Senate. March 15.

Carter G. Woodson, scholar and historian, born in New Canton, Virginia. Dec. 19.

Booker T. Washington graduated from Hampton Institute.

1876 E. M. Bannister, Negro painter, exhibited and received first prize for his "Under the Oaks" at the Philadelphia Centennial Exposition. July 4.

Edward A. Bounchet received the Doctor of Philosophy degree in physics at Yale University, the first Negro awarded the doctorate by an American university.

"Bert" Williams, described by *Billboard* as "the greatest comedian on the American stage" in the early 1900's, born in the Bahamas.

1877 Meta Vaux Fuller, noted female sculptress of the 19th Century, born. June 9.

Henry O. Flipper, born a slave in Georgia, was the first Negro graduate from West Point. June 15.

Frederick Douglass appointed Marshal of the District of Columbia by President Rutherford B. Hayes.

Reconstruction ended with the withdrawal of all Union troops from the South.

1879 William Lloyd Garrison died. May 24.

Blanche K. Bruce presided over the United States Senate. Feb. 15.

1871   William Pickins, orator, author and equal rights fighter, born. Jan. 15.

Frederick Douglass appointed Recorder of Deeds for the District of Columbia. May 17.

Booker T. Washington began his work at Tuskegee Institute. July 4.

1882   Mrs. Violette A. Johnson, first Negro woman admitted to practice before the United States Supreme Court, born. July 16.

Benjamin Brawley, social historian, born. April 22.

Charlotte Hawkins Brown, founder of the Palmer Institute at Sedalia, North Carolina, born.

John F. Slater Fund of one million dollars was created for education and uplifting the Negro in the South.

Robert Morris, first Negro to practice in the courts of the United States, died. Dec. 11.

First Jim Crow railroad car law passed in Tennessee—beginning of modern segregation movement as other Southern states followed.

1883   Shoe lasting machine patented by Jan Matzeliger, American Negro inventor. March 20.

Spellman College organized in basement of church in Atlanta, Georgia. April 11.

Ernest Everett Just, biologist known for research in marine eggs, born. Aug. 14.

Sojourner Truth died in Battle Creek, Michigan. Nov. 26 George Washington Williams wrote a *History of the Negro Race in America,* the first serious history undertaken by a Negro.

1884   The Medico-Chirugical Society of the District of Columbia, oldest American Negro medical society, organized. April 24.

John Roy Lynch, former Congressman, was elected temporary chairman of the Republican convention, the first

Negro to preside over deliberations of a national political party. June 3.

Robert Brown Elliott, Reconstructionist, died. Aug. 9.

William Wells Brown died in Cambridge, Massachusetts.

1886 The first electric trolly on the American continent was run by a Negro, L. Clark Brooks. May 24.

George Washington Cable published a frank treatment of Negro problems in *The Silent South*.

William Whipper, underground railroad leader, died.

1888 Slavery in Brazil abolished. May 14.

1889 Provident Hospital was incorporated in Chicago with the first training school for Negro nurses. Jan. 23.

Asa Philip Randolph, labor leader, born in Crescent City, Florida. April 15.

Frederick Douglass appointed United States Minister to Haiti.

1891 Peter Jackson, great Negro boxer, fought sixty-one round draw with James J. Corbett. May 21.

1892 Luther P. Jackson, Negro historian, born in Lexington, Kentucky. July 11.

Lynchings in the United States reached their peak.

1893 Walter Francis White, long-time Executive Secretary of the NAACP, born in Atlanta, Georgia. July 1.

Dr. Daniel Hale Williams performed the world's first successful heart operation at Chicago's Provident Hospital. July 9.

1895 Frederick Douglass died in Anacosta Heights, District of Columbia, where his home is now a national shrine. Feb. 20.

Booker T. Washngton delivered his famous "Atlanta Compromise" address at Cotton Exposition in Atlanta, Georgia. Sept. 18.

William Grant Still, orchestral musician and composer ("Afro-American Symphony") born. May 11.

Charles E. Houston, considered one of the great constitutional lawyers in American history, born.

W.E.B. Du Bois received his doctorate degree from Harvard University, the first Negro to receive this degree from Harvard. June.

Ida B. Well compiled the first statistical pamphlet on lynching, *The Red Record.*

1896 United States Supreme Court decision of *Plessy v. Ferguson* upheld doctrine of "separate but equal." May 18.

National Association of Colored Women organized in Washington, D.C. by Dr. Mary Church Terrell. July 21.

W.E.B. Du Bois' *The Suppression of the African Slave Trade* was published as the first volume in the Harvard Historical Studies Series.

Booker T. Washington received the first honorary degree awarded to a Negro by Harvard University.

1897 H. A. Rucker served as Collector of Internal Revenue in Georgia. Nov. 4.

John Mercer Langston of Virginia, soldier, educator, Haitian consul, Congressman, died. Nov. 15.

1898 Blanche K. Bruce died in Washington, D.C. March 17.

Bob Cole's *A Trip to Coontown*, was the first musical comedy written by a Negro for Negro talent.

The North Carolina Mutual Life Insurance Company was organized by John Merrick and Dr. A. M. Moore in Durham, North Carolina.

1899 Edward Kennedy ("Duke") Ellington born in Washington, D.C. April 4.

1900 Louis Armstrong born in New Orleans. July 4.

James Augustine Healy died in Portland, Maine. Aug. 5.

Charles W. Chestnutt published his first novel, *The House Behind the Cedars.*

1901 Hiram R. Revels died in Holy Springs, Mississippi. Jan. 16. William M. Trotter founded the *Boston Guardian,* a militant newspaper which advocated absolute equality for Negroes.

1903 Countee Cullen, distinguished Negro poet of the twenties, born. May 30.
W.E.B. Du Bois published his *Souls of Black Folk.*

1904 Dr. Charles R. Drew, "Father of Blood Plasma," born. June 3.
Dr. Ralph J. Bunche born in Washington, D.C. Aug. 7.

1905 Group of Negro intellectuals organized the so-called Niagra Movement at a meeting near Niagara Falls. July 11-13.
Robert S. Abbott began publication of the *Chicago Defender,* the most influential and militant Negro newspaper.

1906 Paul Laurence Dunbar the poet died in Dayton, Ohio. Feb. 9.
The Atlanta race riot resulted in the death of twelve people. Sept. 22.
Alpha Phi Alpha, the first Negro Greek letter society was organized as a fraternity. Dec. 4.

1907 Alaine L. Locke of Harvard was the first American Negro Rhodes Scholar.
Jack Johnson defeated Tommy Burns for the heavy-weight championship at Sydney, Australia.

1908 Thurgood Marshall born in Baltimore, Maryland. Nov. 29.

1909 NAACP founded on Lincoln's birthday after a savage Springfield, Illinois, lynching. Feb. 12.
Commander Robert E. Perry reached the North Pole ac-

companied by his "Negro assistant," Matthew H. Henson. April 6.

Miss Caroline Phelp-Stokes of New York, created a fund for the education of Negroes, died.

Nannie Burroughs founded the National Training School for Women at Washington, D.C.

1910 W.E.B. Du Bois started *Crisis* as the official organ of the NAACP.

National Urban League organized in New York City. April.

1912 W. C. Handy published the first blues composition, *Memphis Blues*. Sept. 27.

1913 Harriet Tubman died in Auburn, New York. March 10.

1914 Joe Louis (Barrow) born in Lexington, Alabama. May 13. The Spingarn Medal awards were instituted by Joel E. Spingarn, Chairman of the Board of Directors of the NAACP, to call to the attention of the American people the existence of distinguished merit and achievement among colored Americans.

1915 Professor Ernest E. Just received the first Spingarn Medal for researches in the field of biology. Feb. 12.

Guinn v. United States declared "grandfather clauses" in the Maryland and Oklahoma constitutions null and void. June 21.

Association of the Study of Negro Life and History founded by Dr. Carter G. Woodson. Sept. 9.

Booker T. Washington died in Tuskegee, Alabama. Nov. 14.

Private Stephen Little, Co. L. 12th Infantry, killed in action, Nogales, Arizona; military camp named in his honor. Nov. 26.

Dr. Robert Russa Moton elected principal, Tuskegee Normal and Industrial Institute. Dec. 20.

About 2,000,000 Southern Negroes moved to Northern industrial centers after the "great migration" began in this year.

1916 Major Charles Young received Spingarn Medal for services in Liberia. Feb. 22.

1917 United States entered World War I.

Harry T. Burleigh, composer, pianist, signer, awarded Spingarn Medal for excellence in the field of creative music. May 16.

Julius Rosenwald Fund for Education, Scientific and Religious Purposes was organized. Oct. 30.

Six hundred Negroes were commissioned officers during World War I.

Edward A. Johnson first Negro to be elected to the New York State Assembly. Nov. 23.

Emmett J. Scott was appointed special assistant to the Secretary of War.

1918 William Stanley Braithwaite, poet, literary critic and editor, received Spingarn medal for distinguished achievement in literature. May 5.

National Liberty Congress of Colored Americans petitioned Congress to make lynching a federal crime. July 29.

First soldiers in American army to be decorated for bravery in France were two Negroes, Henry Johnson and Needham Roberts.

1919 First Pan African Congress, organized by W.E.B. Du Bois, met at Grand Hotel in Paris. Feb. 19-21.

Archibald K. Grimke, former U.S. Consul in Santo Domingo, author and president of the NAACP branch in the District of Columbia for seventy years, received the Spingarn Medal for distinguished service to his race and country. June 27.

There were eighty-three lynchings, the KKK held more than two hundred public meetings across the country, and

there were twenty-five major race riots in the country this
year.

1920 W.E.B. Du Bois awarded Spingarn Medal for his achievements in scholarship, as editor of *Crisis,* and for founding
and calling of the Pan African Congress. June 1.

National Convention of Marcus Garvey's Universal Im-
provement Association opened in Liberty Hall in Harlem;
Garvey's black nationalist movement reached its peak
during this year. Aug. 1.

Emperor Jones, by O'Neill, opened at the Provincetown
Theatre starring Charles Gilpin in the title role. Nov. 3.

1921 Charles S. Gilpin, actor, received the Spingarn Medal for
his performance in the title role of Eugene O'Neill's drama,
Emperor Jones. June 30.

Marcus Garvey inaugurated provisional president of the
"Republic of Africa." Aug. 31.

The doctor of philosophy degree was awarded for the first
time to Negro women: Evan B. Dykes, English at Rad-
cliffe; Sadie T. Mossell, Economics at the University of
Pennsylvania; Georgiana R. Simpson, German at the University of Chicago.

1922 Colonel Charles Young died in Liberia. Jan. 7.

Congress passed the Dyer Anti-Lynching Bill. Jan. 26.

Mary B. Talbert, former president of the National Association of Colored Women, awarded Spingarn Medal for service to the women of her race and the restoration of the
Frederick Douglass home. June 20.

Frederick Douglass Memorial Home in Washington, D.C.
dedicated as museum. Aug. 12.

1923 Spingarn Medal awarded to George Washington Carver,
head of the Department of Research, and director of the
Experiment Station at Tuskegee Institute, Alabama, for
distinguished research in agricultural chemistry. Sept. 4.

First Catholic seminary for the education of Negro priests

33

was dedicated in Bay St. Louis, Mississippi. Sept. 16.

United States Department of Labor estimated that almost 500,000 Negroes left the South during the previous twelve months. Oct. 24.

Charles S. Johnson began to edit *Opportunity: A Journal of Negro Life* for the Urban League.

1924   Roland Hayes, singer, given Spingarn Medal for his great artistry through which he "so finely interpreted the beauty and charm of the Negro folk song" and won for himself a place as soloist with the Boston Symphony Orchestra. July 1.

Fletcher Henderson, first musician to make name with jazz band, opened at Roseland Ballroom on Broadway. October 3.

1925   Charles Drew of Washington, D.C. won Amherst College Ashley Grid Trophy for being most valuable member of the 1924 squad. Jan. 1.

Adelbert H. Roberts elected to Illinois state legislature— first Negro since reconstruction days. Jan. 10.

Greenwood, Mississippi, ministers and prominent business-men led mob which lynched two Negroes. March 14.

Countee P. Cullen, New York University poet, awarded honorary Phi Beta Kappa key. March 28.

Mob at Oscella, Louisiana, flogged and shot minister for "preaching equality." April 18.

A. Philip Randolph organized Brotherhood of Sleeping Car Porters, a labor union. May 8.

Harry T. Burleigh honored by Temple Emmanuel Congregation of New York City at end of 25th year as soloist. May 16.

James Weldon Johnson, former U.S. consul in Venezuela and Nicaragua, former editor, secretary, NAACP, poet, received Spingarn Medal for distinguished achievements as author, diplomat and public servant. June 30.

Louis Armstrong recorded first of "Hot Five and Hot

34

Seven" recordings which influenced jazz. Nov. 11.

1926 Spingarn Medal to Carter G. Woodson, historian and founder of the Association for the Study of Negro Life and History, for ten years' devoted service in collecting and publishing the records of the Negro in America. June 29.
Dr. William S. Scarborough, scholar and educator, died.
Aug. 9.

1927 United States Supreme Court struck down law in Texas
barring Negroes from voting "white primary." March 7.
Anthony Overton, businessman, given Spingarn Medal for
his successful business career climaxed by the admission
of his company as the first Negro organization permitted
to do insurance business under the rigid requirements of
the State of New York. June 28.

1928 Charles W. Chestnutt, author, awarded Spingarn Medal
for his "pioneer work as a literary artist depicting the life
and struggle of Americans of Negro descent, and for his
long and useful career as scholar, worker and freeman in
one of America's greatest cities." July 3.
Oscar de Priest was first Negro from non-Southern state
to be elected to Congress. Nov. 6.

1929 Martin Luther King, Jr. born in Atlanta, Georgia. Jan. 15.
Brotherhood of Sleeping Car porters received charter from
AFL. Feb. 23.
Mordecai Wyatt Johnson, president of Howard University,
received Spingarn Medal "for his successful administration
as first Negro president of the leading Negro university in
America, and especially for his leadership in securing,
durng the past year, legal authority for appropriations to
Howard University by the government of the United
States." July 2.
W. T. Francis, appointed American consul to Liberia by
President Coolidge, died in Africa. July 15.
There were ten known lynchings in the United States dur-
ing the year; Florida led with four.

Francis E. Rivers first Negro admitted to the New York Bar Association.

1930 *Green Pastures* opened on Broadway featuring Richard B. Harrison as "De Lawd." Feb. 26.

Spingarn Medal to Henry A. Hunt, principal for Fort Valley High and Industrial School "for twenty-five years of modest, faithful, unselfish and devoted service in the education of colored people of rural Georgia and the teaching profession in that state." May 3.

The New York *Times* announced that the "n" in "Negro" would hereafter be capitalized. June 7.

Mrs. Mary McLeod Bethune was selected as one of the fifty leading women of America compiled by contemporary social historian Ida Tarbell. June 22.

Joel E. Spingarn elected President of NAACP.

Charles Gilpin, noted actor, died.

Jack Thompson became welterweight champion of the world when he defeated Jackie Fields. May 9.

1931 Richard B. Harrison received Spingarn Medal for his "fine and reverent characterization of the Lord in Marc Connelly's play, *The Green Pastures* (which) has made that play the outstanding dramatic accomplishment in the year 1931. But the Medal is given to Mr. Harrison not simply for this crowning accomplishment, but for the long years of his work as dramatic reader and entertainer, interpreting to the mass of colored people in church and school the finest specimens of English drama from Shakespeare down. It is fitting that in the sixty-seventh year of his life he should receive widespread acclaim for a role that typifies and completes his life work." March 22.

The *cause celebre* trial of the decade, the Scottsboro trial, began in Alabama. April 6.

Dr. Daniel Hale Williams, founder of Chicago's Provident Hospital, died. Aug. 4.

1932 Spingarn Medal to Robert Russa Moton, principal of

Tuskegee Institute, "for his thoughtful leadership of conservative opinion and action on the Negro in the United States, as shown in the U.S. Veterans' Hospital controversy at Tuskegeee; by his stand on education in Haiti; by his support of equal opportunlty for the Negro in the American public school system; and by his expression of the best ideals of the Negro in his books, *What the Negro Thinks*. May 20.

1933 NAACP made its first attack on segregation and discrimination in education and filed suit against the University of North Carolina on behalf of Thomas Hocutt; case was lost on technicality. March 15.

Max Yergan, for ten years American Y.M.C.A. secretary among the native students of South Africa, received the Spingarn Medal as "a missionary of intelligence, tact and self-sacrifice, representing the gift of cooperation and culture which American Negroes may send back to their Motherland; and he inaugurated last year an unusual local movement for interracial understanding among black and white students." July 1.

1934 Mississippi Senate passed a law permitting a private citizen, one C. W. Collins, to spring the trap to hang three Negroes accused of raping Collins' daughter. March 10.

Spingarn Medal to William Taylor Buwell Williams, dean of Tuskegee Institute, "for his long service as field agent of the Slater and Jeanes Funds and the General Education Board, his comprehensive knowledge of the field of Negro education and educational equipment, and his sincere efforts for their betterment." June 29.

Arthur Mitchell defeated Oscar de Priest for the Illinois Congressional seat held by the latter. Nov. 7.

Dr. W.E.B. Du Bois resigned as editor of the *Crisis*.

Bishop W. Sampson Brooks, founder of Monrovia College in Liberia, died in San Antonio, Texas.

1935 Richard B. Harrison died in New York City. March 18.

Joe Louis defeated Primo Carnera at Yankee Stadium. June 25.

Spingarn Medal to Mrs. Mary McLeod Bethune, founder and president of Bethune-Cookman College, Daytona Beach, Florida. "In the face of almost insuperable difficulties she has, almost single-handedly, established and built up Bethune-Cookman College. . . In doing this she has not simply created another educational institution. Both the institution's and Mrs. Bethune's influence have been nationwide. That influence has always been on a high plane, directed by a superb courage. Mrs. Bethune has always spoken out against injustice, in the South as well as in the North, without compromise or fear." June 28. Maryland Court of Appeals ordered University of Maryland to admit Donald Mung. Nov. 5.

National Council of Negro Women founded in New York City with Mrs. Mary McLeod Bethune as president. Dec. 5.

1936   John Hope, president of Atlanta University, winner of the Spingarn Medal. Characterized by the Committee of Award as "a distinguished leader of his race, one of the foremost college presidents in the United States, widely and favorably known throughout the educational world." July 3.

Jesse Owens won four gold medals at the Berlin Olympics. Aug. 9.

NAACP filed first suits in campaign to equalize teachers' salaries and educational facilities. Dec. 8.

1937   William H. Hastie confirmed as judge of Federal District Court in Virgin Islands, thereby becoming the first Negro federal judge. March 26.

Joe Louis defeated James J. Braddock in Chicago for the heavyweight boxing championship of the world. June 22.

Walter White, executive secretary of the NAACP, won the Spingarn Medal for his personal investigation of 41 lynchings and 8 race riots and for his "remarkable tact, skill and persuasiveness" in lobbying for a federal anti-lynching bill. July 2.

Death of Bessie Smith in Clarksdale, Mississippi. Sept. 26.

Bishop Isaac Lane died at the age of 103.

1938   James Weldon Johnson died. June 24.

First woman Negro legislator, Crystal Bird Fauset of Philadelphia, elected to the Pennsylvania House of Representatives. Nov. 8.

United States Supreme Court ruled that states must provide equal educational facilities within its boundaries. Dec. 12.

No Spingarn Medal awarded this year.

1939   Broadway opening of *Mamba's Daughter* gave Ethel Waters her greatest stage triumph. Jan. 14.

D. E. Howard received a patent for his invention of "an optical apparatus for indicating the position of a tool." Jan. 24.

University of Wisconsin refused gift whose donor limited use of funds to white students only. Feb. 18.

Mrs. Franklin D. Roosevelt resigned from the organization of Daughters of Revolution when Marian Anderson was barred from singing in Constitution Hall in Washington, D.C. March.

Marian Anderson gave her Easter Sunday Open Air recital in Washington, D.C.

NAACP launched drive to obtain one million signatures on anti-lynch petition. April 22.

Mississippi Senator Theodore C. Bilbo introduced "Back to Africa Bill" in the United States Senate. April 23.

Joe Louis knocked out Tony Galento in the 4th round. June 28.

Spingarn Medal to Marian Anderson, contralto, ". . . has been chosen for her special achievement in the field of music. Equally with that achievement, which has won her world-wide fame as one of the greatest singers of our

39

time, is her magnificent dignity as a human being. Her unassuming manner, which has not been changed by her phenomenal success, has added to the esteem not only of Marian Anderson as an individual but of the race to which she belongs." July 2.

J. Matilda Bolin appointed first Negro woman judge in the United States; she was made judge of the Court of Domestic Relations in New York City by Mayor Fiorello La Guardia. July 22.

NAACP Legal Defense and Educational Fund organized as separate organization. Oct. 11.

1940 Richard Wright's *Native Son* was published and became one of the best-sellers of the year. Feb.

Virginia legislature chose "Carry Me Back to Ole Virginia" by Negro composer James A. Bland as the state song. April.

Marcus Garvey died in London. June 10.

Louis T. Wright, surgeon, awarded Spingarn Medal "for his contributions to the healing of mankind and for his courageous, uncompromising position held often in the face of bitter attack, that Negro men of medicine should measure up to the most absolute standards of technical excellence and, as a corollary, that having done so, Negro medical men and nurses should be accorded every opportunity to serve, without discrimination on account of race or color." July 19.

Benjamin Oliver Davis, Sr. was appointed Brigadier General, the first Negro general in the history of the American armed forces. Oct. 16.

1941 George Washington Carver awarded the honorary Doctor of Science degree at the University of Rochester. June 18.

United State Supreme Court ruled in railroad Jim Crow case brought by Congressman Arthur Mitchell that separate facilities must be *substantially* equal. April 28.

Richard Wright, author, received Spingarn Medal because "he has given to Americans who have eyes to see a pic-

ture which must be faced if democracy is to survive . . .
For his powerful depiction in his books, *Uncle Tom's Children* and *Native Son,* of the effect of proscription, segregation and denial of opportunities on the American Negro."
June 27.

President Franklin D. Roosevelt established a Fair Employment Practices Commission. July 19.

Dorie Miller of Waco, Texas, messman on USS "Arizona," manned machine gun during Pearl Harbor attack and downed four enemy planes; later awarded Navy Cross. Dec. 7.

1942   Group of Negro and white men and women committed to direct non-violent action organized the Congress of Racial Equality in Chicago. June.

Bernard W. Robinson, Harvard Medical student, made an ensign in the United States Naval Reserve and was first Negro to win a Commission in the United States Navy. June 18.

Spingarn Medal to A. Phillip Randolph, labor leader, international president of the Brotherhood of Sleeping Car Porters, "for his unparalleled record of leadership in the field of labor organization and national affairs for a period of more than three decades . . . in recognition of the dramatic culmination of his years of effort in the mobilization of Negro mass opinion in 1941 in a March on Washington to exercise the constitutional right of citizens of a democracy to petition their government peaceably for the redress of grievances/which/was instrumental in securing the issuance on June 25, 1941, by the President of the United States of an executive order banning discrimination on account of race, creed, color, or national origin in defense industries and in the federal government, and creating the Committee on Fair Employment Practices to effectuate the order. July 19.

William L. Dawson elected to Congress from Chicago. Nov. 3.

1943　Death of George Washington Carver in Tuskegee, Alabama. Jan. 5.

George Gerhswin's *Porgy and Bess* opened on Broadway starring Anne Brown and Todd Duncan. Feb. 28.

Booker T. Washington was the first American merchant ship commanded by a Negro captain, High Malzoc, launched at Wilmington, Delaware.

William H. Hastie, jurist and educator, awarded Spingarn Medal "for his distinguished career as a jurist and as an uncompromising champion of equal justice. His every act, and particularly his protest against racial bigotry in an army fighting for the democratic processes, has established a standard of character and conduct." June 6.

Race riot in Detroit. Thirty-four killed; federal troops called out. June 16.

Major race riot broke out in Harlem. Aug. 1-2.

Lt. Charles Hall, Brazil, Indiana, was first American Negro to shoot down Nazi plane. July 2.

1944　United States Supreme Court in *Smith v. Allwright*, banned the "white primary" which had effectively prevented Negros in the South from voting. April 24.

United Negro College Fund established. April 24.

Dr. Mary E. Branch, president of Tillotson College, Austin Texas, died. July 8.

Spingarn Medal awarded to Dr. Charles R. Drew, scientist, "for his outstanding work in blood plasma. Dr. Drew's research in this field led to the establishment of a blood plasma bank which served as one of the models for the widespread system of blood banks used by the American Red Cross. Dr. Drew was appointed full-time Medical Director for the blood plasma project for Great Britain. The report on this work was published and served as a guide for later developments for the United States Army and for the armies of our Allies." July 16.

Death of composer Will Marion Cook. July 20.

Negro historian Edward A. Johnson died. July 24.

Adam Clayton Powell elected first Negro Congressman from the East. Aug. 1.

Anna Lucasta, starring Hilda Simms and Frederick O'Neil, opened on Broadway and was one of the year's great stage successes. Aug. 20.

SS*Frederick Douglass,* first ship named for a Negro, was sunk by enemy action. Aug. 20.

Negro servicewomen sworn into WAVES for first time. Dec. 13.

1945   First state Fair Employment Practices Commission was established in New York State. March 12.

One thousand white students walked out of Gary, Indiana, schools to protest school integration. Sept. 18.

Paul Robeson, singer and actor, received Spingarn Medal for "distinguished achievement in the theatre and on the concert stage." Oct. 18.

Irving C. Molleson, Chicago Republican, sworn in as United States Customs Judge. Nov. 3.

More than one million Negroes were inducted or drafted into the United States armed forces by the time World War II ended.

1946   Countee Cullen, poet, died in New York City. Jan. 9.
William H. Hastie confirmed as governor of the Virgin Islands. May 1.

Mrs. E. C. Clement first Negro named "Mother of the Year." May 1.

Supreme Court banned segregation in interstate bus travel. June 3.

Thurgood Marshall, special counsel of the NAACP, given Spingarn Medal for "his distinguished service as a lawyer before the Supreme Court of the United States and inferior courts, particularly in the Texas Primary Case, which conceivably may have more far-reaching influence than any other act in the ending of disfranchisement based upon race or color in the country." June 28.

1947   Jackie Robinson joined the Brooklyn Dodgers, first Negro in organized baseball in modern times. April 10.

Dr. Percy L. Julian, research chemist, received the Spingarn Medal "in recognition of his work as a distinguished chemist who has made many important discoveries that have saved many lives. He has demonstrated technical skill, courage and sustained effort on the highest level in making contributions that will benefit mankind for years to come." June 27.

President's Committee on Civil Rights condemned racial injustices in America in a formal report, "To Secure These Rights." Oct. 29.

1948   First Lt. Nancy C. Leftenant was first Negro accepted in the regular Army Nurse Corps. Feb. 12.

United States Supreme Court declared restrictive housing covenants unenforceable in the courts (*Shelly. v. Kraemer*) May 3.

Negro elected for the first time to the American Nurses' Association Board of Directors. June 12.

A. Philip Randolph formed the League for Non-Violent Civil Disobedience Against Military Segregation. June 26.

Spingarn Medal awarded to Channing H. Tobias, "in recognition of his consistent role as a defender of fundamental American liberties . . . He brought to the President's Committee on Civil Rights intellectual vitality, courage and the richness of his long experience in the field of race relations. Largely due to his persistence and clear insight the committee produced a report of historic significance in man's unending struggle for justice." June 27.

Poet Claude McKay died in Chicago.

1949   Congressman William L. Dawson became Chairman of House Expenditures Committee, the first Negro to head a standing Committee in Congress. Jan. 18.

Palisades, New Jersey, swimming pool integrated after two-year non-violent campaign. June 1.

Wesley A. Brown was first Negro to graduate from Annapolis Naval Academy. June 3.

United States Navy Department announced policy of equality of treatment and opportunity to all persons in Navy and Marine Corps. June 7.

Dr. Ralph J. Bunche, international civil servant, awarded Spingarn Medal "for his distinguished scholarship in the Myrdal study, his painstaking efforts as director of the United Nations Trusteeship Division, but principally for his priceless contribution to the settlement of armed conflict in the Middle East." June 17.

Station W E R D was opened as the first Negro-owned radio station in the United States in Atlanta, Georgia. Oct. 3.

William H. Hastie nominated for United States Circuit Court of Appeals. Oct. 15.

Famed dancer Bill Robinson of stage and screen died in New York City. Nov. 25.

1950   James Weldon Johnson Memorial Collection of Negro Arts and Letters given to Yale University by Charles Van Vechten. Jan. 8.

Dr. Charles R. Drew, pioneer in blood research, died. April 1.

Death of Dr. Carter G. Woodson in Washington, D.C. April 3.

Attorney-General MacGrath and Solicitor-General Perlman argued before the U.S. Supreme Court for the reversal of 1896 ruling which upheld segregation. April 4.

Charles H. Houston, leading constitutional lawyer, died. April 22.

While holding against segregation in the three cases before it, the U.S. Supreme Court avoided general ruling on "separate but equal" doctrine. June 6.

Spingarn Medal awarded posthumously to Charles H. Houston, Chairman, NAACP Legal Committee and "stalwart defender of democracy, inspired teacher of youth, and leader in the legal profession . . . in memory of a lifetime of gallant championship of equal rights for all Americans, of unselfish devotion to democratic ideals, of unswerving fidelity to the American dream of equal opportunity." June 25.

American Medical Association seated first Negro delegate. June 26.

Mrs. E. Sampson was first United States Negro appointed as representative to the United Nations. Aug. 19.

Dr. Ralph J. Bunche was the first American Negro to receive the Nobel Peace Prize. Sept. 22.

Althea Gibson filed entry for national tennis championship; first Negro accepted. Oct. 26.

1951 National Association of Colored Graduate Nurses disbanded since aim to integrate Negroes into nursing profession achieved. Jan. 27.

University of North Carolina admitted first Negro student in its history. April 24.

Oscar De Priest, former Congressman from Illinois, died. May 12.

Dr. Ralph J. Bunche first Negro to win honorary degree from Princeton, New Jersey. June 13.

Spingarn Award to Mabel Keaton Staupers, who, as a leader of the National Association of Colored Nurses, "spearheaded the successful movement to integrate Negro nurses into American life as equals," and whose work was "characterized by wisdom, vision, courage and refusal to equivocate," as a result of which the NACGN was dissolved as no longer needed. June 29.

Carver National Monument in Joplin, Missouri dedicated; first national park honoring Negro. July 14.

Harry T. Moore, NAACP Coordinator for Florida, killed by bomb blast in house. Dec. 27.

Pfc. W. H. Thompson given Medal of Honor posthumously for Korean War action; first Negro to receive this since Spanish-American War.

Riots in Cicero, Illinois, worst since 1919.

Martin Luther King, Jr. received the Bachelor of Divinity degree from Crozier Theological Seminary, Chester, Pennsylvania.

1952 University of Tennessee admitted its first Negro student. Jan. 12.

Judge Waring quit his Charleston, South Carolina home as result of ostracism for his fight for Negroes. Feb. 24.

Spingarn Medal awarded posthumously to Harry T. Moore, NAACP leader in the State of Florida and a martyr in the "crusade for freedom," for "his invaluable contributions and his courage in working for full implementation of the democratic ideal," including justice in the courts, the abolition of segregation at the University of Florda, and the expansion of the Negro vote in the state. Assassinated by a hate bomb in his home at Mims on Christmas night, 1951. June 27.

Ford Theatre of Baltimore dropped segregation policy in effect since 1861.

Southern Regional Council reported forty bombings since January 1951. Dec. 7.

Tuskegee Institute reported that 1952 was the first year in seventy-one years of tabulation that there were no reported lynchings. Dec. 30.

1953 Fisk was first Negro institution of higher education in United States to get Phi Beta Kappa chapter. April 5.

United States Supreme Court ruled that District of Columbia restaurants could not legally refuse to serve Negroes. June 8.

Albert W. Dent of Dillard University was elected President of the National Health Council. June 20.

NAACP set integregation as goal, dropped "separate but equal" theory. June 23.

Paul R. Williams, distinguished architect, awarded Spingarn Medal for his pioneer contributions as a creative designer of livable and attractive modern dwellings and beautiful utilitarian commercial structures—contributions which have won for him the respect and admiration of his fellow architects and high rank in his chosen profession. June 26.

Drama by Negro playwright Louis Peterson, *Take a Giant Step*, opened on Broadway. Sept. 24.

Hulan Jack elected president of the Borough of Manhattan. Nov. 4.

1954 J. Ernest Wilkins of Chicago appointed Assistant Secretary of Labor by President Dwight Eisenhower. April 23.

Landmark United States Supreme Court case, *Brown v. Board of Education, et al.* declared that racial segregation in public schools was unconstitutional. May 17.

White Brotherhood set up in Georgia to retain segregation. June 6.

E. L. Ashford of Pacific Coast League was first Negro umpire in organized baseball. June 13.

Spingarn Medal to Theodore K. Lawless, physician, educator, and philanthropist, recognized as one of the world's leading dermatologists, for his extensive research and experiments which have enlarged the area of scientific knowledge in his chosen field. July 4.

First White Citizens Council unit was organized in Indianola, Mississippi. July 11.

Charles V. Bush was first Negro page boy in Supreme Court and first in Capitol page school. July 24.

Mary Church Terrell died in Washington, D.C. July 24.

Dr. F. M. Snowden appointed cultural attache in embassy in Rome; first Negro in major embassy post. Aug. 19.

S. Richardson named Chairman of the Federal Parole Board; first Negro on Board. Sept. 29.

Benjamin Davis, Jr. appointed first Negro general in the Air Force. Oct. 27.

Defense Department announced all units in the armed forces were now integrated. Oct. 30.

Carol Williams engaged by Sadler Wells Opera. Nov. 26.
Track star M. Whitman first Negro to win Sullivan Trophy,
top United States amateur award. Dec. 31.

1955   Marian Anderson made her debut at the Metropolitan
Opera House; she was the first Negro singer in the company's history. Jan. 7.

Charlie Parker, one of the founders of the modern jazz
movement, died. March 12.

Death of Walter White, NAACP leader, in New York City.
March 21.

Roy Wilkens appointed Executive Secretary of NAACP.
April 11.

Mrs. Mary McLeod Bethune died in Daytona Beach,
Florida. May 18.

U.S. Supreme Court decree for the implementation of
the May 17, 1954, school desegregation decision; "with all
due deliberate speed." May 31.

Spingarn Medal awarded to Carl Murphy, dedicated
editor, publisher and far-sighted civic leader, for his
leadership role in leveling invidious racial barriers in
employment, education and recreation. June 26.

E. F. Morrow appointed administrative officer in the
Eisenhower Executive Office. July 8.

Georgia Education Board ordered lifetime ban on teachers
who instructed "mixed" classes. July 11.

Emmet Till, fourteen years old, was kidnapped and
lynched in Money, Mississippi. Aug. 28.

Interstate Commerce Commission banned segregation in
buses, waiting rooms and travel coaches involved in interstate travel. Nov. 25.

Bus boycott initiated in Montgomery, Alabama. Dec. 5.

1956   Autherine Lucy admitted to University of Alabama. Feb. 3.
National Press Club admitted L. R. Lautier as first Negro.
Feb. 5.

Miss Lucy suspended after riot at University of Alabama. Feb. 7.

Manifest denouncing U.S. Supreme Court ruling on segregation in public schools was issued by one hundred Southern Senators and Representatives. March 11-12.

U.S. Supreme Court banned segregation in public parks, playgrounds, beaches and golf courses; rejected "separate but equal" doctrine.

Leontyne Price was first Negro to sing before mixed audience in Laurel, Mississippi.

Louisville, Kentucky, schools integrated. Sept. 10.

Dr. Hohn Hope Franklin appointed chairman of the history department at Brooklyn College.

Jack ("Jackie") R. Robinson, brilliant and versatile athlete, received Spingarn Medal for "his superb sportsmanship, his pioneer role in opening up a new field of endeavor for young Negroes, and his civic consciousness." Dec. 8.

1957　Martin Luther King, Jr. elected president of Southern Christian Leadership Conference at its organization meeting in New Orleans. Jan. 12.

Robert Ming, Chicago lawyer, elected Chairman of American Veterans Committee, first Negro to head major national veterans organization. April 28.

Spingarn Medal awarded to Martin Luther King, Jr., dedicated and selfless clergyman, for his creative contributions to the Fight for Freedom and his outstanding leadership role in the successful Montgomery bus protest movement. June 28.

Althea Gibson won women's Single Championship at Wimbledom, England and the United States Lawn Tennis Championship. July 7, 22.

Booker T. Washington National Monument opened at Rocky Mount, Virginia; second such memorial to a Negro leader. July 28.

Rev. A. J. Carey, Jr. appointed Chairman of President's

Government Employment Policy Committee; first Negro in this position. Aug. 6.

Prayer Pilgrimage, the largest civil rights demonstration staged by American Negroes up to that time, held in Washington, D.C.

Congress passed the first Civil Rights Act since 1875. Aug. 29.

President Eisenhower ordered federal troops to Little Rock, Arkansas, to prevent interference with school integration at Central High School. Sept. 24.

New York City was first to legislate against racial or religious discrimination in housing with the adoption of its Fair Housing Practice law. Dec. 5.

1958   Clifton R. Wharton confirmed as Minister to Rumania. Feb. 5.

Mrs. Daisy Bates and the Little Rock Nine awarded Spingarn Medal for "their pioneer role in upholding the basic ideals of American democracy in the face of continuing harassment and constant threats of bodily injury." July 11.

Members of NAACP Youth Council began series of sit-ins at Oklahoma City lunch counters. Aug. 19.

1959   First play written by a Negro woman, *Raisin in the Sun*, by Lorraine Hansberry, was one of the major Broadway hits. March 11.

Second "Youth March for Integrated Schools" drew 30,000 students to Washington, D.C. April 18.

Mack Parker lynched in Poplarville, Mississippi. April 25. Prince Edward County, Virginia, Board of Supervisors abandoned public school system in attempt to prevent school segregation. June 26.

Rev. Dr. King and others urged President Eisenhower to make statement against segregation. July 5.

Billie Holiday, leading blues singer, died in New York City. July 17.

Dade County, Florida, first to desegregate public schools in Florida.

Spingarn Medal given to Edward Kennedy (Duke) Ellington, composer and orchestra leader, for his outstanding musical achievements which have won for him "not only universal acclaim but also worldwide recognition of our country's contribution to the field of music." Sept. 11.

Citizens of Deerfield, Illinois, authorized plan which blocked building of interracial housing development. Dec. 21.

1960 Forty-three arrested in Raleigh, North Carolina, sit-in. Feb. 10.

Fifty-nine arrested in Chatanooga, Tennessee, sit-in. Feb. 19.

Pope John elevated Bishop Laurian Rugambwa of Tanganyika to College of Cardinals, first Negro Cardinal in modern times. March 3.

Students served at Salisbury, North Carolina and at Atlanta, Georgia, lunch counters; students demonstrated in New Orleans. March 7.

Three hundred and fifty protestors arrested and placed in stockade in Orangeburg, South Carolina. March 15.

Forty arrested in sit-ins in four North Carolina cities. March 17.

Thirty-seven Negroes arrested in public libraries in Memphis Tennessee. March 19.

Twenty-three arrested in art gallery and library in Memphis. March 22.

Lunch counters integrated in Corpus Christi, Texas; sixteen students arrested in Baton Rouge, Louisiana. March 28.

Ten arrested in Birmingham sit-in; White House Conference on Children and Youth endorsed sit-ins. March 31. Student Non-Violent Coordinating Committee organized on Shaw University campus. April 15.

Sit-in protest at chain stores in Savannah, Georgia; fifteen

arrested picketing chain stores in
April 16.

United States Federal Court rule
must start school segregation by S
Winston-Salem lunch counters in

Four lunch counters integrated in
June 4.

Langston Hughes, poet, author a
Spingarn Medal in recognition
America, Europe, Asia, Africa, Ce
as a major American writer and
poet laureate of the Negro race."

Democratic National Conventic
plank supporting sit-ins and sch
Elijah Muhammad, black inter
for creation of Negro state at
July 31.

Southern Regional Council repo
desegregated lunch counters ma
Southern School News reported
America were attending segreg

During decade of 1950-1960, 1,
from South to Northern commu

Richard Wright died in Paris. N

1961 Adam Clayton Powell assumed
Education and Labor Committ
sentatives. Jan. 3.

Carl T. Rowan appointed Dep
State for Public Affairs. Jan. 2:

H. Lewis conducted Los Angel
first Negro to conduct major
home during the regular seasor

Robert Weaver sworn in as Ad
Home Finance Agency, highes
an American Negro. Feb. 11

53

irteen "Freedom Riders" began bus trip through the
uth. May 4.

prano Leontyne Price starred in Metropolitan Opera
mpany's *Girl of the Golden West,* first Negro to open
et season in leading role. May 24.

arvin Cook named ambassador to Niger Republic; first
gro envoy named by Kennedy Administration to African
tion. May 26.

F. Poole appointed U.S. Attorney for Northern Cali-
rnia District; first Negro in such position appointed in
ntinental United States. April 16.

cksonville, Florida, closed its swimming pool to avoid
tegration. June 13.

ne Baker, former 2nd baseman for Pittsburgh Pirates,
s first Negro ex-major leaguer to advance to position
major league farm team. June 20.

n "Freedom Riders" sentenced in Tallahassee Airport
se. June 23.

eorge L. P. Weaver named Secretary of Labor in charge
international affairs. July 9.

ingarn Medal awarded to Kenneth B. Clark, Professor
Psychology at the College of the City of New York;
under and director of the Northside Center for Child
evelopment and prime mobilizer of the resources of
odern psychology in the attack upon racial segregation,
r his dedicated service and inspired research which con-
ibuted significantly to the historic U.S. Supreme Court
cision of May 17, 1954, banning segregation in public
lucation. July 16.

esident John F. Kennedy nominated Thurgood Marshall
the United States Circuit Court of Appeals. Sept. 23.

tis Marion Smith became Associate Justice on the Michi-
n Supreme Court. Oct. 10.

incinnati Reds outfielder, Frank Robinson, voted "Most
aluable Player" of the year by Baseball Writers' Associa-
n. Nov. 23.

James H. Meredith registered at the University of Mississippi.

United Press International picked Chicago Cubs' outfielder, Billy Williams, as the National League's "Rookie of the Year."

Ernie Davis of Syracuse University was first Negro to win Harmon Trophy as college football's "Player of the Year."

American Anthropological Association reaffirmed belief in inherent equality of Negroes and whites. Nov. 21.

Negroes comprised 12% of population in cities of over 1,000,000, compared with 10% of a decade ago. Dec. 3.

In a final blow to "massive resistance," United States courts held unconstitutional a law permitting closing of integration-ordered public school districts.

There was an increase of 17,907 students, or 6%, in the South's Negro attendance of mixed classes over 1960.

School board presidencies of Oakland, California, and Washington, D. C. went to Negroes, the first Negroes to lead school systems in major United States metropolitan centers.

John Duncan became first Negro to serve as Commissioner for Washington, D.C.

Chicago Human Relations Commission reported city's Negro population rose from 492,265 to 812,637, in the decade from 1950 to 1960.

1960 Census showed that 1,087,931 Negroes resided in New York City; 14% of city's total population and the largest number of Negroes of any city in the United States.

1962   Jackie Robinson was first Negro to be elected to National Baseball Hall of Fame. Jan. 24.

Lt. Commander Samuel L. Gravely given command of destroyer escort, USS *Falgout;* first Negro to command U.S. warship. Jan. 31.

Mattiwilda Dobbs became first person (Negro or white) to sing before integrated audience in Municipal Hall in Atlanta, Georgia. Feb. 1.

John Thomas appointed Director of the Health, Education and Welfare Department's Cuban Refugee Program. March 15.

Census Bureau reported 6,025,173 of 18,871,831 Negroes lived in 25 largest cities; 1,457,000 Negroes migrated from South to northern and western regions in last decade. April 15

Johnson Publishing Company was first Negro company to enter book publishing field. April 25

Luke C. Moore became first U.S. Marshal since Frederick Douglass held such position. May 9.

John Hope Franklin appointed William Pitt Professor of American History and Institutions at Cambridge University, England, for one year. May 20

Death of E. Franklin Frazier, noted sociologist and historian, after 45 years of teaching. May 22

J. O'Neill named Chicago Cubs coach; first Negro coach in major leagues. May 30

W. S. Braithwaite, poet, anthologist and literary critic, died in New York City. June 9

Big Bill Russell of the Boston Celtics named "Player of the Year" by Sporting News. June 19

NAACP had more cases before the U.S. Supreme Court than any institution except the federal government. June 18

Rev. W. E. Houston was first Negro elected Moderator of United Presbyterian Church, N. Y. Synod. June 21

Robert C. Weaver, Administrator, Housing and Home Finance Agency, awarded Spingarn Medal for his long years of dedicated public service at municipal, state and federal levels; for his pioneer role in the development and advocacy of the doctrine of "open occupancy" in housing; and for his responsible and militant leadership in the struggle for human rights. July 8

Rev. Martin Luther King, Jr. arrested in Albany, Georgia, after anti-segregation demonstration. July 10

Howard Jenkins, law professor at Howard University, appointed first Negro member of the National Labor Relations Board. July 22

Mel Goode was first Negro TV news commentator on network TV (ABC-TV). Aug. 29

U. S. Supreme Court ruled that University of Mississippi must admit James H. Meredith, a Negro Air Force veteran, whose application for admission had been on file for 14 months. Sept. 10

Hobart Taylor, Jr. appointed Executive Vice-Chairman of the President's Equal Opportunity Committee. Sept. 11

Mississippi Governor Ross R. Barnett personally denied James H. Meredith admission to University of Mississippi. Sept. 20

U. S. Circuit Court of Appeals ordered Board of Higher Education of Mississippi to admit Meredith to the University or face contempt charges; Board agreed to comply with order. Sept. 24

Governor Barnett defied orders of Court and personally interfered with Meredith's attempt to enter the University to register. Sept. 25

A. Leon Higginbotham nominated as federal judge for eastern Pennsylvania, youngest member of the federal bench in the U.S. Sept. 26

Thurgood Marshall confirmed as member of Second United States Circuit Court of Appeals after one year delay by Southern opposition in U.S. Senate. Sept. 12

Four major TV advertisers approved use of Negro models in commercials aimed at nation-wide audience.

James Meredith escorted to the campus of the University of Mississippi with Federal Marshals. Sept. 30.

University of Mississippi students and adults from Oxford, Mississippi, and other Southern communities rioted on campus; two killed.

Federal soldiers restored order on campus and in town. Oct. 1

Accompanied by federal marshals, James Meredith registered at the University. Oct.

Edward W. Brooke elected Attorney General of Massachusetts. Nov. 7

August Hawkins elected as U.S. Representative from California, first Negro to represent this state. Nov. 7

Leroy Johnson first Negro state legislator elected in Georgia since Reconstruction. Nov. 8

Gerald Lamb elected Connecticut State Treasurer. Nov. 8

U.S. Supreme Court ruled that segregation in interstate and intra state travel was unconstitutional.

Diahnn Caroll was first Negro to play romantic lead in an otherwise all-white Broadway musical, Richard Rodgers *No Strings*. April 15.

Maury Wills of the Los Angeles Dodgers broke all records in major league baseball as the greatest "baseball thief" (stolen bases).

Wilt Chamberlain of the San Francisco Warriors was first professional basketball player to score 4000 points in a single season.

2000 Negroes were enrolled in previously "whites only" colleges and universities in the South.

There were 948 "token-integrated" public school districts in the all-white southern school districts, an increase of 124 districts over 1961.

Archbishop Joseph F. Rummel directed all Roman Catholic schools in his Louisiana archdiocese to integrate.

Marjorie Lawson became first Negro woman judge in Washington, D.C.

Mrs. Ann Roberts appointed FHA Deputy Regional Administrator and became highest ranking Negro woman in the federal housing field.

Fourteen Southern airports voluntarily integrated their passenger facilities.

The Albany (Georgia) Movement, comprising the civil rights efforts of several action groups, including CORE,

SNCC, SCLC, and the NAACP resulted in the following achievements in social relations: (1) agreement by local authorities to form a bi-racial committee on racial problems; (2) desegregation of the city's bus terminal and cafe; (3) release from jail of movement demonstrators and an end to mass arrests; (4) the substitution of "Mr. & Mrs." for derogatory terms by city officials in addressing Negro citizens.

U.S. Supreme Court authorized Tennessee citizens to sue in federal courts to force reapportionment of legislative districts. This would result in shift of political power from rural segregationist strongholds to the relatvely more liberal, heavily Negro-populated urban South.

1963   James Baldwin's *The Fire Next Time* published. Jan. 31
President John F. Kennedy sent his Civil Rights Message to Congress. March 1

Carl T. Rowan appointed Ambassador to Finland. March 9

John Thomas appointed Director of the Health, Education, and Welfare Department's Cuban Refugee Program. March 15

Dr. John Hope Franklin appointed to the faculty of the University of Chicago. April 14

Arthur Ashe, 19, was first Negro to join the U.S. Davis Cup Tennis Team. May 14

U.S. Supreme Court ruled that in cities making segregation a matter of public policy, whether by ordinance or executive order, Negroes may not be prosecuted for seeking service in privately owned stores. May 21

President Kennedy said nation faced "moral crisis" over Negro demands for equality; pledged legislation to open public facilities for all (TV address). June 12

Spingarn Medal awarded to Medgar Wile Evers, NAACP Field Secretary for the State of Mississippi, World War II veteran, hero and martyr felled by an assassin's bullet in the back on June 12; accepted posthumously by his wife. July 4

Largest civil rights demonstration in history took place at the site of the Lincoln and Washington Memorial in Washington, D. C.; 250,000 persons participated. Aug. 29

Bomb exploded in Birmingham Negro Baptist Church killing four Negro girls; two Negro youths killed in racial rioting which followed. Sept. 6

James W. Silver, Professor of History at the University of Mississippi and retiring President of the Southern Historical Association, charged that Mississippi is "a closed society and a century behind culturally." Nov. 8

Rev. Benjamn J. Anderson, pastor of Princeton's historic Witherspoon Street Presbyterian Church, was nominated to become the first Negro to serve as a moderator of the General Assembly of the United Presbyterian Church. Nov. 30

Ralph J. Bunche and Marian Anderson were among the recipients of Medals of Freedom from President L. B. Johnson at the White House. Dec. 7

Dinah Washington died. Dec. 14

Outfielder Tommy Davis of the Los Angeles Dodgers won baseball's batting crown for the 2nd consecutive year.

William T. Mason Jr. appointed first Negro Assistant Federal Attorney in Virginia.

1964   Senator Barry Goldwater called public accommodations section of the Civil Rights Act unconstitutional. Jan. 19

Carl T. Rowan appointed Director of the United States Information Agency, the highest position ever held by a Negro in the federal government. Jan. 21

Atlanta *Constitution,* a leading Southern newspaper, reversed a previous position and editorially supported the public accommodations provision of the Civil Rights Act. Jan. 22

Beckworth trial for murder of Medgar Evers opened. Feb. 1

A. T. Walden sworn in as Atlanta municipal judge; first Negro judge in Georgia since Reconstruction. Feb. 4

Mistrial in Beckworth trial; jury unable to agree. Feb. 8

Race riot in Jacksonville, Florida. March 24-26

U.S. Supreme Court set aside contempt conviction of Negro Mary Hamilton who declined to answer in Alabama court when addressed as "Mary." March 31

Second jury unable to agree in Beckworth case; mistrial declared. April 26

U.S. Supreme Court ruled that Prince Edward County in Virginia must re-open its public schools on an integrated basis. May 26

Sidney Poitier won the Academy of Motion Picture Arts and Sciences' Oscar Award as best actor of 1963 for his performance in *Lilies of the Field*. April

Three civil rights workers reported missing on Mississippi Summer Project two weeks after release from jail in Philadelphia, Mississippi. June 23

Spingarn Medal awarded to Roy Wilkens, Executive Secretary of the NAACP, "despite his own urgent request that this present honor not be conferred upon him," for the "distinctive and immeasurable contribution to the advancement of the American people and the national purpose" in his work on behalf of civil rights movement. June 23

Race riots in Rochester, New York. July 1

Civil Rights Act of 1964 passed and signed into law; most far-reaching civil rights legislation since Civil War Amendments. July 3

Fifteen year old Negro James Powell shot and killed by off-duty police Lt. Gilligan in New York City. July 17

Race riot in Harlem. July 19

Bodies of civil rights workers Goodman, Schwerner and Chaney found in newly-built earthen dam near Philadelphia, Mississippi. Aug. 5

Race riots in South Chicago suburb in Dixmoor; 50 hurt. Aug. 17-18

Philadelphia race riots; 29 hurt. Aug. 29-30.

FBI arrested four Philadelphia, Mississippi, law enforcement officers and former sheriff in connection with murder of three civil rights workers. Oct. 4

Rev. Martin Luther King, Jr. won Nobel Peace Prize. Oct. 15

NAACP resumed operations in Alabama for first time since enjoined from operating in state in 1956. Nov. 1

Negro Baptist Church burned near Ripley, Mississippi. Nov. 1

Civil Rights struggle in Mississippi has resulted in: three killed, eighty beaten, three wounded by gunfire, over one thousand arrested, thrty-five churches burned, thirty-one homes and other buildings bombed—since the beginning of the year 1964.

Jackson District Attorney announced Beckwith will not be tried for murder of Medgar Evers without new evidence. Nov. 15

U.S. Supreme Court upheld the constitutionality of the public accommodations section of the Civil Rights Act of 1964. Dec.

Public schools of the District of Columbia were registering a pupil enrollment of 85.7% Negro.

Ford Foundation announced grants totalling $15,000,000 to strengthen Negro colleges.

Hampton Institute opened its new Communications Center, marking the 125th anniversary of the birth of the founder of Hampton, Samuel C. Armstrong.

Senator Richard B. Russell (Georgia) proposed a voluntary relocation of Negroes proportionately at government expense throughout the states of the federal union.

Arthur B. Spingarn, a founder of NAACP and President since 1940, announced plans to retire at the end of the year.

Erwin S. Perry, who received his Ph D. this year from the University of Texas, made such a distinguished record that he was appointed to the University faculty commencing in September.

Mrs. E. D. Koontz was elected President of the NEA's Department of Classroom Teachers; first Negro to hold presidency in this, the largest professional organization in the United States. July 5

Hobart Taylor appointed Associate Special Counsel at the White House for President L. B. Johnson, succeeding Theodore C. Sorenson.

National Urban League launched anti-poverty campaign among Negroes under leadership of Whitney Young, Jr.
Clinton E. Knox nominated Ambassador to Dahomey.

John Haynes Holmes, one of founders of NAACP, died.

Three Broadway shows included interracial romances without audience incident: *Golden Boy, A Sign in Sidney Brustein's Window, The Owl and the Pussy Cat.*

Negro athletes contributed significantly to United States prestige at the XVIII Olympics in Tokyo by winning half of the 36 gold medals awarded American athletes.

1965 Three men indicted for beating Negro rights worker in Greenwood, Mississippi, were the first three to be arrested under the Civil Rights Act of 1964.

Survey of N. Y. *Times* of compliance with Civil Rights Act showed substantial compliance with Title II (Public Accommodations) in South, but "painfully slow progress against voting discrimination under Title I."

Geraldine McCullough became the first Negro winner of the Widener Memorial Medal for Sculpture, awarded by the Pennsylvania Academy of Fine Arts.

United States Supreme Court reversed trespass convictions of two Negroes for refusing to leave Enfield, North Carolina, restaurant in 1960; Court cited earlier decision that the Civil Rights Act abated pending state prosecutions for peaceful demonstrations.

Malcolm X assassinated in New York City while addressing rally of his followers.

B. O. Davis was nominated for rank of Lieutenant General of the United States Air Force, the highest rank ever reached by a Negro in the military service.

The first Negro city councilman in the history of San Antonio, Texas, was elected when Rev. S. H. James defeated three candidates.

St. Thomas Episcopal Church of Philadelphia voted to nullify its 1796 charter restriction that limited membership to "Africans and descendants of African race."

Lawrence W. Bradford, Jr., 16, of New York City, and Frank W. V. Mitchell, 15, of Springfield, Illinois, were appointed as first Negro page boys in Congress.

Soprano Leontyne Price was awarded the Order of Merit of the Italian Republic.

Bill Russell of the Boston Celtics was named the most valuable player in the National Basketball Association for the 4th time in 5 years.

Mrs. Crystal Bird Fauset, pioneer female legislator, died.

Bob Hayes was voted outstanding male track and field athlete of 1964 by the National Academy of Sports.

J. Raymond Jones elected leader of the powerful New York County Democratic Committee (Tammany Hall).

Lorraine Vivian Hansberry, leading Negro playwright, died in New York City.

Seven foot two inch Ferdinand Lewis Alcindor, Jr., 18, viewed as the "next Wilt Chamberlain," announced his choice of the University of California at Los Angeles for his college academic and basketball career.

Leonard Bennet, Jr., a Senior Editor of *Ebony* Magazine, was awarded the 1965 Patron Saints Award Society of Midland Authors for his biography of Dr. Martin Luther King, Jr., *What Manner of Man.*

Nat King Cole, noted singing artist, died in Los Angeles.

Dorothy Cross was hired by the Kentucky Education Association as its first Negro professional worker.

Jimmie Lee Jackson, wounded while attempting to protect his mother from being beaten by an Alabama State Trooper in rioting which followed police invasion of a voter registration rally in Marion, Alabama, died in a Selma hospital.

Bishop Prince A. T. Taylor, Jr., became the first Negro to assume the presidency of the Council of Bishops of the Methodist Church.

President Johnson issued Executive Order creating cabinet-level Council on Equal Opportunity, with Vice-President Humphrey as Chairman, to coordinate civil rights activities of all federal agencies.

Reverend James J. Reeb died as a result of a beating inflicted upon him by 4 white racists in Selma, Alabama.

Rev. Reeb, a white Unitarian minister from Boston, had gone to Selma to participate in the voter registration demonstrations there.

President Johnson, in televised address to Congress, called for immediate action on voters rights legislation; he pledged that "we shall overcome crippling legacy of bigotry and injustice."

Federal Judge authorized Selma-Montgomery march.

President Johnson called up almost 4,000 troops to protect Selma-Montgomery marchers.

Rev. Dr. King, Under-Secretary Bunche, lead 3,200 beginning 54 mile Selma-Montgomery march.

March from Selma ended as 25,000 Negroes and whites rallied in front of capitol, Montgomery.

Mrs. Viola Liuzzo shot to death while driving between Selma and Montgomery. Mrs. Liuzzo went to Alabama to participate in the Selma-to-Montgomery march.

Brief

Selected Bibliography On

The American Negro

Aptheker, Herbert, *American Negro Slave Revolts,* Columbia University Press, 1943. An account of early attempts by Negroes to win their freedom.

Aptheker, Herbert. *A Documentary History of the Negro People in the United States.* Citadel Press, 1951. A collection of hundreds of documents covering American Negro history through 1910.

Bone, Robert A. *The Negro Novel in America.* Yale University Press, 1958. Traces the development of the Negro novel from 1890 to the present.

Bontemps, Arna W. *The Story of the Negro.* Knopf, 1948. A general, although elementary, survey of the Negro from Africa to the New World.

Bontemps, Arna and Conroy, Jack. *They Seek A City.* Doubleday, 1945. A study of the internal migrations of Negroes, especially movements toward New York, Chicago and Detroit.

Brown, Ina C. *The Story of the American Negro.* Friendship Press, 1957. Broad history of the Negro's life in America. African background is particularly well done.

Butcher, Margaret Just. *The Negro in American Culture,* Knopf, 1956. The Negro as a "catalyst of American democracy."

Buckmaster, Henrietta. *Let My People Go,* Harper, 1941. The story of the Underground Railroad.

Carter, Hodding. *The Angry Scar,* Doubleday, 1959. A modern view of the Reconstruction years.

Cornish, Dudley I'. *The Sable Arm: Negro Troops in the Union Army,* Longmans, 1956. The role of the Negro in the Civil War brilliantly told.

Du Bois, William E. B. *Black Reconstruction.* Saifer, 1952. Classical 'revisionist" study of a much-distorted period in American history.

Franklin, John Hope. *From Slavery to Freedom,* Knopf, 1956. The most complete, scholarly survey of American Negro history now available.

Furnas, Joseph C. *The Road to Harper's Ferry,* Sloane, 1959. The Negro from Africa to John Brown's raid.

Handlin, Oscar. *The Newcomers,* Harvard University Press, 1959. A study of Negroes and Puerto Ricans in New York City.

Johnson, Charles S. *The Negro in American Civilization.* Henry Holt, 1930. An older but valuable overview of Negro history in the 1920's and just before the New Deal.

Hughes, Langston and Meltzer, Milton. *A Pictorial History of the Negro in America.* Crown, 1956. A history told in text and illustrations.

Konvitz, Milton R. *A Century of Civil Rights.* Columbia University Press, 1961. History of civil rights in the United States with specific relation to Negroes.

Logan, Rayford W. *The Negro in American Life and Thought: The Nadir. 1877-1901.* Dial Press, 1954. The period thoughtfully surveyed.

Myrdal, Gunnar. *An American Dilemma.* 2 Vols. Harper, 1944. The most authoritative study of the Negro in contemporary America.

Quarles, Benjamin. *The Negro in the American Revolution.* University of North Carolina Press, 1961. First full-scale account of the Negro in the American Revolution. Revealing and inspiring.

Redding, J. Saunders. *They Came In Chains.* Lippincott, 1950. Well-written presentation of the American Negro through American history.

Simkins, Francis B. *A History of the South.* Knopf, 1953. A history of the South which accurately records the role played by the Negro.

Thorpe, Earl E. *The Mind of the Negro,* Ortlieb Press, 1961. The most recent work available dealing with Negro intellectual history.

Stamp, Kenneth M. *The Peculiar Institution,* Knopf, 1956. Thorough, unbiased study of Negro slavery in the South. Destroys myths.

Woodson, Carter G. *Negro In Our History,* Associated Publishers, 1959. Excellent basic volume on general history of the Negro.

Tables

NEGRO COLLEGES AND UNIVERSITIES

States and Institutions	Location	Year Founded	Denominational Connection	Enrollment
Alabama:				
Alabama A.&M. College	Normal	1875	Non-sect.	1100
Alabama State Teachers College	Montgomery	1874	Non-sect.	1205
Daniel Payne College	Birmingham	1889	A.M.E.	(N)*
Lomax-Hannon College	Greenville	1893	A.M.E.Z.	(N)
Miles College	Birmingham	1907	C.M.E.	(N)
Oakwood College	Huntsville	1896	Seventh Day adv.	(N)
Selma University	Selma	1878	Baptist	(N)
Stillman College	Tuscaloosa	1876	Pres. U.S.A.	385
Talladega College	Talladega	1867	Cong. Christian	336
Tuskegee Institute	Tuskegee	1881	Non-sect.	1790
Arkansas:				
A.M.&N. College	Pine Buff	1873	Non-sect.	1396
Arkansas Baptist College	Little Rock	1884	Baptist	(N)
Dunbar Junior College	Little Rock	1929	Non-sect.	(N)
Morris Booker Baptist College	Dermott	1934	Baptist	(N)
Philander Smith College	Little Rock	1868	Methodist	798
Shorter College	N. Little Rock	1886	A.M.E.	231
Delaware:				
Delaware State College	Dover	1891	Non-sect.	294
District of Coulmiba:				
Howard University	Washington	1867	Non-sect.	3375
Miner Teachers College	Washington	1851	Non-sect.	574
Florida:				
Bethune-Cookman College	Daytona Beach	1904	Methodist	624
Edward Waters College	Jacksonville	1866	A.M.E.	635
Florida A.&M. College	Tallahassee	1887	Non-sect.	2424
Florida N.&I. Memorial College	St. Augustine	1892	Baptist	289
Washington Junior College	Pensacola	1949	Non-sect.	(N)
Georgia:				
Albany State College	Albany	1903	Non-sect.	625

* (N) Not reported.

States and Institutions	Location	Year Founded	Denominational Connection	Enrollment
Atlanta University	Atlanta	1867	Non-sect.	394
Clark College	Atlanta	1869	Methodist	773
The Fort Valley State College	Fort Valley	1895	Non-sect.	793
Georgia Baptist College	Macon	1899	Baptist	(N)
Morehouse College	Atlanta	1867	Baptist	730
Morris Brown College	Atlanta	1881	A.M.E.	743
Paine College	Augusta	1883	Methodist & C.M.E.	336
Savannah State College	Savannah	1890	Non-sect.	833
Spelman College	Atlanta	1881	Baptist	427

Kanses:

Kansas City Kansas Junior College	Kansas City	1923	Non-sect.	388

Kentucky:

Kentucky State College	Frankfort	1886	Non-sect.	585
Louisville Municipal College	Louisville	——	Non-sect.	244

Louisiana:

Dillard University	New Orleans	1933	Methodist Cong.	869
Grambling College	Grambling	1901	Non-sect.	2590
Leland College	Baker	1870	Baptist	132
Southern University and A&M College	Baton Rouge	1880	Non-sect.	1,883
Xavier University	New Orleans	1925	R.C.	1,014

Maryland:

Carver Junior College	Rockville	1950	Non-sect.	28
Coppin State Teachers College	Baltimore	1900	Non-sect.	353
Maryland State Teachers College	Bowie	1866	Non-sect.	309
Maryland State College	Princess Ann	1886	Non-sect.	346
Morgan State College	Baltimore	1867	Non-sect.	1,913

Mississippi:

Alcorn A.&M. College	Alcorn	1871	Non-sect.	753
Campbell College	Jackson	1890	A.M.E.	80
Jackson College	Jackson	1877	Baptist	1,447
Mary Holmes Junior College	West Point	1892	Presb. USA	67
Mississippi Industrial College	Holly Springs	1905	C.M.E.	501
Mississippi Vocational College	Itta Bena	1950	Non-sect.	638
Okolona College	Okolona	1902	Prot. Epis.	102
Piney Woods School (Jr. College)	Piney Woods	1910	Non-sect.	86
Prentiss N&I Institute	Prentiss	1907	Non-sect.	72
Rust College	Holly Springs	1866	Methodist	371
Southern Christian Institute	Edwards	1875	Disciples of Christ	87
Tougaloo College	Tougaloo	1869	Cong.	435

70

States and Institutions	Location	Year Founded	Denominational Connection	Enrollment
Missouri:				
Harriet Beecher Stowe Teachers College	St. Louis	1890	Non-sect.	535
Lincoln Junior College	Kansas City	1936	Non-sect.	80
Lincoln University	Jefferson City	1866	Non-sect.	999
Western Baptist Seminary	Kansas City	1889	Baptist	(N)
North Carolina:				
A.&T. College of N. Carolina	Greensboro	1891	Non-sect.	2,501
Barber-Scotia College	Concord	1867	Preb. USA	230
Bennett College	Greensboro	1873	Methodist	466
Elizabeth City State Teachers College	Elizabeth City	1891	Non-sect.	477
Fayetteville State Teachers College	Fayetteville	1887	Non-sect.	587
Immanuel Lutheran College	Greensboro	1903	Lutheran	36
Johnson C. Smith University	Charlotte	1867	Presb.	664
Livingstone College	Salisbury	1879	A.M.E.Z.	468
North Carolina College	Durham	1910	Non-sect.	1,390
St. Augustine College	Raleigh	1867	Prot. Epis.	437
Shaw University	Raleigh	1865	Baptist	579
Winston-Salem Teachers College	Winston-Salem	1892	Non-sect.	900
Ohio:				
Central State College	Wilberforce	1887	Non-sect.	997
Wilberforce University	Wilberforce	1856	A.M.E.	294
Oklahoma:				
Langston University	Langston	1897	Non-sect.	564
Pennsylvania:				
Lincoln University	Lincoln Univ.	1854	Non-sect.	350
State Teachers College	Cheyney	1837	Non-sect.	572
South Carolina:				
Allen University	Columbia	1870	A.M.E.	820
Benedict College	Columbia	1870	Baptist	727
Bettis Academy & Junior College	Trenton	1881	Mt. Canaan Educ. & Miss. Assn.	(N)
Claflin University	Orangebury	1869	Methodist	375
Clinton N.&I. College	Rock Hill	——	A.M.E.Z.	(N)
Friendship Junior College	Rock Hill	1891	Baptist	200
Harbison Junior College	Irmo	1882	Presb. USA	(N)
Morris College	Sumter	1908	Baptist	324
State A.&M. College	Orangeburg	1896	Non-sect.	1,194
Voorhees School & Junior College	Denmark	1897	Prot. Epis.	116
Tennessee:				
Fisk University	Nashville	1865	Non-sect.	747

71

States and Institutions	Location	Year Founded	Denominational Connection	Enrollment
Knoxville College	Knoxville	1875	Presb.	513
Lane College	Jackson	1882	C.M.E.	397
LeMoyne College	Memphis	1870	Cong. Christian A.M.E. Assn.	410
Morristown N.&I. College	Morristown	1881	Methodist	233
Swift Memorial Junior College	Rogerville	1883	Presb. USA	(N)
Tennessee State University	Nashville	1919	Non-sect.	3,000
Texas:				
Bishop College	Marshall	1880	Baptist	575
Butler College	Tyler	1905	Bapt. Miss.	201
Conroe N.&I. College	Conroe	1903	Baptist	(N)
Jarvis Christian College	Hawkins	1912	Disciples of Christ	217
Mary Allen Senior College	Crockett	1886	Baptist	91
Paul Quinn College	Waco	1872	A.M.E.	292
Prairie View A.&M. College	Prairie View	1876	Non-sect.	2,372
St. Philip's Junior College	San Antonio	1898	Non-sect.	(N)
Samuel Houston College	Austin	1876	Methodist	(N)
Texas College	Tyler	1894	C.M.E.	385
Texas Southern University	Houston	1947	Non-sect.	1,097
Tillotson College	Austin	1877	Cong. Christian	(N)
Wiley College	Marshall	1873	Methodist	698
Virginia:				
Hampton Institute	Hampton	1868	Non-sect.	1,211
St. Paul's Polytechnic Institute	Lawrenceville	1888	Episcopal	(N)
Virginia State College	Petersburg	1882	Non-sect.	(N)
Virginia Theological Seminary and College	Lynchburg	1888	Baptist	(N)
Virginia Union University	Richmond	1865	Baptsit	868
West Virginia:				
Bluefield State College	Bluefield	1895	Non-sect.	516
Storer College	Harpers Ferry	1867	Baptist	(N)
W. Virginia State College	Institute	1891	Non-sect.	2,233

NEGRO ORGANIZATIONS

Alpha Kappa Alpha Sorority — °f: 1908   m: 40,000
to encourage high scholastic and ethical standards, promote unity among college women and to be of service to mankind.

Alpha Kappa Mu Honor Society — f: 1937   m: 6,680
encourage high scholarship among college undergraduates and scholarly achievement among the alumni.

Alpha Phi Alpha Fraternity — f: 1906   m: 8,000
to develop a strong unit of college trained men dedicated to social uplift and progress through education, active citizenship and the creation of a climate of good-will.

American Teachers Association — f: m: 37,000
to provide equal educational opportunities for all children and equality of professional status for all teachers.

Ancient and Accepted Scottish Rite Masons — f: 1864   m: 20,000
dedicated its program to fraternal and charitable causes, with emphasis on civic and educational activities.

Ancient Egyptian Arabic Order Nobles of the Mystic Shrine — f: m: 24,000
to enhance the work and programs of Prince Hall Masonry, promoting local and national charitable, civic, educational and economic development programs.

Benevolent Protective Order of Reindeer (Women's Auxiliary) — f: 1923   m: 3,000
guided by its cardinal principles of "Service, Unity and Charity," participate in a program designed to implement these objectives.

Bible Way Church of Our Lord Jesus Christ World Wide — f: 1957   m: 50,000
to promote Christian Fellowship, Pentecostal Evangelism, Christian Education and Foreign Home missions.

Chi Delta Mu Fraternity — f: 1913   m: 1,000
to provide a media for better communication between physicians, dentists and pharmacists.

---

f—founded
m—membership

73

Chi Eta Phi Sorority	f: 1932	m: 600

to elevate nursing to a generally higher plane.

The Drifters	f:	m: 150

dedicated to charitable, social, civic and educational interests.

Frontiers International	f: 1936	m: 2,000

service to the community.

Gamma Phi Delta Sorority	f: 1940	m:

to encourage and finance the education and training of women in schools, colleges.

Grand Temple Daughters I.B.P.O.E. of W.	1902	m: 150,000

scholarship aid to deserving youth; participate in international affairs; promote financial assistance for the welfare of war orphans and health charities.

Grand United Order of Odd Fellows	f:	m: 114,000
Improved Benevolent Protective Order of Elks of the World	f: 1898	m: 500,000
Imperial Court Daughters of Isis	f: 1910	m:

to promote benevolent and charitable work.

International Conference of Grand Chapters Order of the Eastern Star	f: 1907	m: 250,000
Jack and Jill	f:	m: 5,000

to aid youth through legislation aimed at bettering conditions for all children.

Kappa Alpha Psi Fraternity	f: 1911	m: 27,000

to unite college men . . . to encourage honorable achievement . . . and to inspire service in the public interest.

Knights of Peter Claver	f: 1909	m: 15,000

to plan, promote and sponsor commendable Catholic works.

Lambda Kappa Mu Sorority	f: 1937	m: 675

to encourage higher education among young women.

Links	f: 1946	m: 2,000

interested in civic activities, intercultural relations and friendship.

National Association for the Advancement of Colored People	f: 1909	m: 400,000

to achieve full equality for the Negro in America.

National Association of Barristers Wives	f: 1949	m:

to promote a closer union and secure a more intimate relationship among the wives of lawyers, and to enhance the prestige of the legal profession.

National Association of College Deans and Registrars	f: 1926	m: 250

shares information of common interest regarding the administration of higher educacation and the promotion of professional welfare among its members.

74

National Association of College
Women

f: 1923   m: 1500
advancement of education, civic activities
and human relations.

National Association of Colored
Women's Clubs

f: m: 100,000
service and education

National Association of Fashion
and Accessory Designers

f: 1950   m: 350

National Association of Market
Developers

f: 1953   m: 150 chapters
to raise the level of ethics and performance
of those connected with the Negro market.

National Association of Ministers'
Wives

f: 1941   m: 1,000
to foster fellowship among ministers' wives
across denominational lines.

National Association of Negro
Business & Prfoessional
Women's Clubs

f: 1935   m: 25,000
to protect the interest of business and
professional women and direct their attention toward united action for improved
social and civic conditions.

National Association of Negro
Musicians

f: 1919   m: 1,000
to aid young people through music scholar-
ships, fostering professional ethics in the
arts and establishing cultural institutions.

National Bankers Association

f: 1926   m:
to encourage the establishment and sound
operation of banks by Negroes.

National Bar Association

f: 1925   m: 2,500
promote the legal profession.

National Beauty Culturists'
League

f: 1919   m: 50,000
to establish more standardized and scientific methods of hair, skin and scalp treatment. Also to raise the standards of the
profession.

National Business League

f: 1900   m:
to stimulate business and to promote the
industrial, commercial and general economic welfare of Negroes.

National Conference of Artists

f: 1959   m:
to improve the position and promulgate
the work of Negro artists in American life.

National Convention of Gospel
Choirs and Choruses

f: 1932   m: 2,500
to elevate the standards of gospel and
spiritual music.

National Council of Negro Women

f: 1935   m: 2,850,000
foster united planning and concerted action
for the economic, social, educational and
cultural welfare of Negro women.

National Dental Association

f: 1913   m: 1,000

National Epicureans

f: 1951   m: 280
to promote the social, cultural, literary,
civic and benevolent interests of its members.

National Funeral Directors and Morticians Association
f: m: 2,000
promotes the art and science of funeral directing.

National Grand Chapter of the Eastern Star
f: m: 10,000
auxiliary of Ancient & Accepted Scottish Rite Masons; charitable activities.

National Insurance Association
f: 1921   m: 11,000
to raise the standards and practices of the participating members.

National Medical Association
f: 1895   m: 4.200
to foster the scientific advancement of medicine.

National Newspaper Publishers Association
f: 1940   m: 50
to evaluate current trends and problems in the newspaper industry.

National Technical Association, Inc.
f: 1926   m: 300
to collect and disseminate information on existing opportunities for Negro youth in technical fields.

National United Church Ushers Association of America
f: 1919   m: 35,000
establishment of a unified system of Church ushering for all Christian churches.

National Urban League
f: 1910   m:
to eliminate segregation and discrimination in American life

Omega Psi Phi Fraternity
f: 1911   m: 10,000
fellowship, scholarship aid, social action and civil rights are foremost on its program of activities.

Phi Beta Sigma Fraternity
f: 1914   m: 12,000
social action, education and scholarship.

Tau Gamma Delta Sorority
f: 1942   m: 500
to cultivate and encourage high scholastic standards.

The Association for the Study of Negro Life and History
f: 1915   m: 2,000
to promote historical research and writing of Negro history.

76

NEGRO POPULATION IN THE UNITED STATES

Definition of "Negro" for census purposes which appears in the Reports of the United States Bureau of the Census:

"A person of mixed white and Negro blood shall be returned as a Negro, no matter how small the percentage of Negro blood. Both black and mulatto persons are to be returned as Negroes, without distinction. A person of mixed Indian and Negro blood shall be returned as a Negro, unless the Indian blood very definitely predominates and he is nuiversally accepted in the community as an Indian. Mixtures of non-white races should be reported according to the race of the father, except that Negro-Indian should be reported as Negro."

Year	Total Population	Negro Population	Percent
1890	3,929,214	757,208	19.3
1800	5,308,483	1,002,037	18.9
1810	7,239,881	1,377,808	19.
1820	9,638,453	1,771,656	18.4
1830	12,866,020	2,328,642	18.1
1840	17,169,453	2,873,648	16.07
1850	23,191,876	3,638,808	15.7
1860	31,443,790	4,441,830	14.1
1870	39,818,449	4,880,009	12.7
1880	50,155,783	6,580,793	13.
1890	62,947,714	7,488,676	11.
1900	75,994,775	8,833,994	11.6
1910	93,402,151	9,827,763	10.7
1920	105,710,620	10,463,131	9.9
1930	122,775,046	11,891,143	9.7
1940	131,669,275	12,865,518	9.8
1950	150,697,361	15,042,286	10.
1960	179,323,175	18,871,831	10.5

NEGRO NEWSPAPERS AND PERIODICALS

Alabama
Anniston. The *Mirror*, c. 2,140
Birmingham. The *Mirror*, c. 14,436
Birmingham. *Birmingham World*,
  c. 9,700
Huntsville. The *Mirror*, c. 3,160
Mobile. Mobile *Beacon*, c. 5,500
Montgomery. Alabama *Tribune*,
  c. 1,500
Sheffield. *Tri-Cities Mirror*, c. 2,235
Tuscaloosa. Alabama *Citizen*, c. 8,000
Tuskegee. *Herald*, c. 2,740

Alaska
Anchorage. Alaska *Spotlight*, c. 1,000

Arizona
Phoenix. Arizona *Sun*, c. 5,500
Phoenix. Arizona *Tribune*, c. 3,000

Arkansas
Little Roc. Arkansas *Survey-Journal*,
  c. 12,550
Little Rock. Arkansas *World*,
  c. 13,560
Little Rock. *State Press*, c. 17,656
Pine Bluff. *Negro Spokesman*, c. 7,000

California
Los Angeles. *California Eagle*,
  c. 27,500
Los Angeles. *Herald-Dispatch*,
  c. 31,000
Los Angeles. *The Sentinel*, c. 29,810
Oakland. California *Voice*, c. 12,500
San Diego. *Comet*, c. 10,000
San Diego. *The Lighthouse*, c. 85,000
San Diego. *The Voice*, c. 12,800
San Francisco. *The Independent*,
  c. 8,096
San Francisco. *Sun Reporter*, c. 8,000

Colorado
Denver. *Colorado Statesman*, c. 2,900
Denver. *Star*, c. 1,200
Pueblo. *Western Ideal*, c. 1,110

District of Columbia
Afro-American (semi-weekly)
  c. 24,753
The Pyramid, c. 22,000
Capitol Times, c. 13,500

Florida
Jacksonville. *Florida Star-News*,
  c. 25,374
Jacksonville. *Florida Tattler*,
  c. 16,500
Miami. *Miami Times*, c. 10,500
Pensacola. *Colored Citizen*, c. 1,100
Pensacola. *Courrier*, c. 5,300
Tampa. *Florida Sentinel-Bulletin*,
  c. 15,000
Tampa. *News Reporter*, c. 4,920
Sarasota. *Weekly Bulletin*, c. 4,500

Georgia
Albany. *Southwest Georgain*, c. 2,900
Atlanta. *Atlanta Daily World*,
  c. 29,500
Atlanta. *Atlanta Inquirer*, c. 18,911
Augusta. *Weekly Review*, c. 4,600
Columbus. *World* (Sundays), c. 2,800
Voldosta. *The Telegram*. c. 10,000

Illinois
Champaign. *Illinois Times*, c. 1,500
Chicago. *Chicago Defender*, c. 31,254
Chicago. *New Crusader*, c. 19,541
East St. Louis. *The Beacon*, c. 3,500
East St. Louis. *The Crusader*,
  c. 7,000
Joliet. *Negro Voice*, c. 4,500
Rockford. *The Crusader*, c. 4,500

Indiana
Evansville. *Consolidated News*
  (bi-weekly) c. 7,000
Gary. *The American*, c. 6,885
Gary. *The Crusader*, c. 4,730
Indianapolis. *Indianapolis Recorder*,
  c. 11,288

Iowa
Des Moines. *Iowa Bystander*, c. 2,592
Des Moines. *Observer*, c. 1,100

Kansas
Kansas City. *Plaindealer*, c. 15,000
Wichita. The *Enlightener*, c. 2,400

Kentucky
Louisville. *Louisville Defender*,
  c. 3,460
Louisville. *Leader*, c. 15,296

Louisiana
Baton Rouge. Baton Rouge *News Leader*, c. 9,800
Alexandria. *News Leader*, c. 10,500
Bossier City. *The Hurricane*, c. 2,375
New Orleans. *Louisiana Weekly*, c. 19,532
Shreveport *Shreveport Sun*, c. 9,800

Maryland
Baltimore. *Afro-American*, c. 60,548

Massachusetts
Boston. *Boston Chronicle*, c. 10,509
Boston. Boston *Roxbury City News*, c. 14,000
Boston. Boston *Graphic*, c. 4,000
Boston. *The Orator*, c. 2,000
Boston. *The Times*, c. 12,000
Boston. *Guardian*, c. 10,000
Springfield. *The Sun.* c. 12,500

Michigan
Detroit. *The Courier*, c. 6,900
Detroit. Michigan *Chronicle*, c. 36,639
Detroit. Michigan *Scene*, c. 4,100
Detroit. *The Tribune*, c. 28,700

Minnesota
Minneapolis. *The Spokesman*, c. 10,416
Minneapolis. *The Twin City Observer*, c. 2,000
St. Paul. *The Recorder*, c. 8,322
St. Paul. *The Sun*, c. 2,000

Mississippi
Greenville. *Delta Leader*, (Sundays) c. 3,000
Jackson. *The Jackson Advocate*, c. 4,000
Jackson. Mississippi *Free Press*, c. 8,000

Missouri
Kansas City. *Kansas City Call*, c. 21,528
St. Louis. The *American*, c. 7,200
St. Louis. The *Argus*, c. 8,761
St. Louis. *Crusader*, c. 5,000
St. Louis. *New Citizen*, c. 3,100
St. Louis. *New Crusader*, c. 4,100

Nebraska
Omaha. *Omaha Star*, c. 5,600
Omaha. *The Guide*, c. 4,050

New Jersey
Asbury Park. *Central Jersey Post*, c. 7,500
Newark, N.J. *Afro-Amercian*, c. 5,925
Newark, N.J. *Herald News*, c. 28,080

New York
Brooklyn. N.Y. *Recorder*, c. 17,750
Buffalo. Buffalo *Empire Star*, c.15,000
Buffalo. *Criterion*, c. 12,000
Rochester. The *American Negro*, c. 7,000
Syracuse. *Progressive World*, c. 9,300
Westchester County. Westchester County *Press*, c. 3,500
Westchester County. Westchester *Observer*, c. 7,500

New York City
N. Y. *Courier*, c. 10,932
N. Y. *Amsterdam News*, c. 89,596

North Carolina
Charlotte. *Charlotte Post*, c. 18,265
Charlotte. *Queen City Gazette*, c. 2,750
Durham. Carolina *Times*, c. 22,100
Greensboro. *Future Outlook*, c. 8,762
Raleigh. The *Carolinian*, c. 6,800
Wilmington. Wilmington *Journal*, c. 11,500

Ohio
Cincinnati. *The Herald*, c. 4,900
Cleveland. *Call & Post*, c. 27,268
Cleveland. The *Courier*, c. 10,747
Columbus. Ohio *Sentinel*, c. 3,862
Hamilton. Butler County *American*, c. 2,650
Toledo. *Bronze Raven*, c. 9,500
Youngstown. *Buckeye Review*, c. 5,500

Oklahoma
Muskogee. Oklahoma *Independent*, c. 1,500
Oklahoma City. *Black Dispatch*, c. 11,688
Tulsa. Oklahoma *Eagle*, c. 6,000

Oregon
Portland. Northwest *Clarion*, c. 15,000

Pennsylvania
Philadelphia. Philadelphia *Afro-American*, c. 6,797
Philadetlphia. *Courier*, c. 4,163

Philadelphia. *Independent,* c. 16,441
Philadelphia. *Tribune,* c. 50,590
Pittsburgh. Pittsburgh *Courrier,*
　c. 15,919

Rhode Island
Providence. *Chronicle,* c. 1,541
South Carolina
Charleston. *New Citizen,* c. 2,000
Columbia. Palmetto *Times,* c. 4,000
Columbia. *Lighthouse & Informer,*
　c. 6,400
Greenville. *American,* c. 2,000
Kingstree. Carolina *Sun,* c. 1,000

Tennessee
Chattanooga. Chattanooga *Observer,*
　c. 4,500
Knoxville. *Flashlight Herald,* c. 3,700
Memphis. The *State Defender,*
　c. 5,648
Memphis. Memphis *World* (semi-
　weekly) c. 6,000
Nashville. Nashville *Commentator,*
　c. 2,500

Texas
Dallas. Dallas *Express,* c. 5,045

Fort Worth. Fort Worth *Weekly,*
　c. 2,000
Fort Worth. Fort Worth *Mind,*
　c. 12,955
Houston. *Informer,* c. 15,171
Houston. Negro *Labor News*
　(Monthly) c. 20,000
Houston. *Sunnyside Digest,* c. 3,000
Houston. *Forward Times,* c. 12,000
San Antonio. San Antonio *Register,*
　c. 9,924
Waco. The *Messenger,* c. 3,400

Virginia
Charlottesville. Charlottesville-
　Albermarle *Tribune,* c. 2,271
Norfolk. *Journal & Guide,* c. 32,190
Richmond. Richmond *Afro-American,*
　c. 15,175
Roanoke. *Roanoke Tribune,* c. 15,300

West Virginia
Bluefield. *Independent Observer,*
　c. 2,400

Wisconsin
Milwaukee, *Gazette,* c. 11,010
Milwaukee. *The Star,* c. 6,000

African Heritage, c. 15,000
African Opinion, c. 3,000 (bi-monthly)
A.M.E. Church Review, c. 5,000
　(quarterly)
Bronze California, c. 30,000
Bulletin of the National Dental Asso-
　ciation, c. 2,000
Crisis (NAACP) N.
Ebony Magazine, c. 825,000
Elegant Magazine, c. 60,000
Freedomways, c. 6,000
Fisk Herald, c. 1,250 (quarterly)
Ivy Leaf, c. 10,000 (quarterly)
Journal of Human Relations, c. 1,200
　(quarterly)
Journal of the National Medical Asso-
　ciation, c. 3,600 (bi-monthly)

Journal of Negro History, c. 5,000
　(quarterly)
Journal of Religious Thought, c. 1,500
Jet Magazine, c. 700,000
Muhammad Speaks, c. 50,000
Negro History Bulletin, c. 8,900
News Illustrated, c. 4,000
Phylon, c. 2,500
Quarterly Review of Higher Education,
　c. 1,000
St. Augustine's Messenger, c. 5,000
The Message Magazine, c. 50,000
Tan Magazine, c. 200,000
The Voice, c. 50,000
Voice of Missions, c. 10,000
Wilberforce Interpreter, c. 4,500
　(quarterly)

The First Civil Rights Act of 1866

An Act to Protect All Persons in the United States in Their Civil Rights, and Furnish the Means of Their Vindication

Be it enacted . . . , That all persons born in the United States and not subject to any foreign power, excluding Indians not taxed, are hereby declared to be citizens of the United States; and such citizens, of every race and color, without regard to any previous condition of slavery or involuntary servitude, except as a punishment for crime whereof the party shall have been duly convicted, shall have the same right, in every State and Territory in the United States, to make and enforce contracts, to sue, be parties, and give evidence, to inherit, purchase, lease, sell, hold, and convey real and personal property, and to full and equal benefit of all laws and proceedings for the security of person and property, as is enjoyed by white citizens, and shall be subject to like punishment, pains, and penalties, and to none other, any law, statute, ordinance, regulation, or custom, to the contrary notwithstanding.

Section 2. And be it further enacted, That any person who, under color of any law, statute, ordinance, regulation, or custom, shall subject, or cause to be subjected, any inhabitant of any State or Territory to the deprivation of any right secured or protected by this act, or to different punishment, pains, or penalties on account of such person having at any time been held in a condition of slavery or involuntary servitude, except as a punishment for crime whereof the party shall have been duly convicted, or by reason of his color or race, than is prescribed for the punishment of white persons, shall be deemed guilty of a misdemeanor, and, on conviction, shall be punished by fine not exceeding one thousand dollars, or imprisonment not exceeding one year, or both, in the discretion of the court.

Section 3. And be it further enacted, That the district courts of the United States, within their respective districts, shall have, exclusively

DATE DUE	
NOV 12 1997	
MAR 30 2000	